Crisco®

DELICIOUS
Desserts for All Occasions

pil
Publications
International, Ltd.

Photography: Stephen Hamilton Photographics, Inc.
Photographers: Stephen Hamilton, Tate Hunt
Photographers' Assistants: Tom Guida, Derek Hatfield
Prop Stylist: Paula Walters
Food Stylists: Chris Ingengno, Josephine Orba
Assistant Food Stylist: Lisa Knych

Pictured on the front cover: Raspberry and Cream Pie *(page 60)* and Frosted Holiday Cut-Outs *(page 11)*.

Pictured on the back cover *(clockwise from left):* Glazed Chocolate Pound Cake *(page 46),* St. Pat's Pinwheels *(page 16)* and Spiced Cranberry-Apple Sour Cream Cobbler *(page 64).*

ISBN: 0-7853-8507-X

Manufactured in China.

8 7 6 5 4 3 2 1

Microwave Cooking: Microwave ovens vary in wattage. Use the cooking times as guidelines and check for doneness before adding more time.

Crisco®

DELICIOUS Desserts for All Occasions

Crisco wants you to have success in the kitchen. That's why Crisco.com, our Crisco cooking community, gives you everything you need to become a great cook! We provide you with valuable content including recipes, tips, meal solutions, and cooking education that will build your confidence and cooking skills so everything you prepare will be a success time after time.

Join our community. It's the perfect place if you've just begun to cook, have a limited repertoire, or want knowledge and support. For those of you more experienced cooks, there's something for you as well. No matter what your cooking background, everyone will find new ideas to add variety to family meals.

As part of the Crisco cooking community, we will also be looking to you to share your recipes and cooking experiences with others. Come explore Crisco.com.

We Cook!

STORING AND FREEZING

Take the guess work out of storing and freezing baked goods. With these simple tips, it has never been easier to plan ahead. Many items can be baked ahead and frozen. A variety of unbaked doughs can also be frozen to be baked up hot and fresh at the last minute.

COOKIES & BARS

Unbaked cookie dough can be refrigerated for up to one week or frozen for up to six weeks. Rolls of dough (for slice-and-bake cookies) should be sealed tightly in plastic wrap; other doughs should be stored in airtight containers. For convenience, label plastic wrap or containers with baking information.

Store soft and crisp cookies separately at room temperature to prevent changes in texture and flavor. Keep soft cookies in airtight containers. If they begin to dry out, add a piece of apple or a slice of bread to the container to help them retain moisture. Store crisp cookies in containers with loose-fitting lids to prevent moisture buildup. Store cookies with sticky glazes, fragile decorations and icings in single layers between sheets of waxed paper.

As a rule, crisp cookies freeze better than soft, moist cookies. However, rich, buttery bar cookies are an exception because they freeze extremely well. Freeze baked cookies in airtight containers or freezer bags for up to six months. Thaw cookies and brownies unwrapped at room temperature.

CAKES

Store one-layer frosted cakes in their baking pans, tightly covered. Store layered frosted cakes under a cake cover or under a large inverted bowl. Cakes with whipped cream frostings or cream fillings should always be stored in the refrigerator.

Unfrosted cakes can be frozen up to four months if well-wrapped in plastic wrap. Thaw them, unwrapped, at room temperature. Frosted cakes should be frozen unwrapped until the frosting hardens, and then wrapped, sealed and frozen for up to two months. To thaw, remove the wrapping and thaw at room temperature or in the refrigerator. Cakes with fruit or custard fillings don't freeze well because they become soggy when thawed.

BREADS & MUFFINS

Quick breads should be wrapped well in plastic wrap and stored at room temperature to stay fresh up to one week. Or, they may be frozen for up to three months wrapped in heavy-duty foil. Muffins should be stored in a sealed plastic food storage bag up to three days. Or, they may be frozen for up to one month wrapped in heavy-duty foil.

PIES

Unbaked pie dough can be frozen for later use. Simply flatten the dough into disks and stack in a freezer bag with waxed paper between the layers.

Meringue-topped pies are best when served the day they are made; leftovers should be refrigerated. Custard or cream pies should be refrigerated immediately after cooling. Fruit pies should be covered and stored at room temperature overnight; refrigerate them for longer storage.

To freeze unbaked fruit pies, do not cut steam vents in the top crust. Cover them with inverted paper plates for extra protection and package in freezer bags or plastic wrap. To bake, do not thaw. Cut slits in the top crust and allow an additional 15 to 20 minutes of baking time. Baked fruit pies can be frozen after they're completely cooled. To serve, let the pie thaw at room temperature for two hours, then heat until warm. Pies with cream or custard fillings and meringue toppings don't freeze well.

Just for Kids

CARAMEL LACE CHOCOLATE CHIP COOKIES

1/4 **Butter Flavor CRISCO® Stick or** 1/4 **cup Butter Flavor CRISCO®**
all-vegetable shortening plus additional for greasing
1/2 **cup light corn syrup**
  1 **tablespoon brown sugar**
1 1/2 **teaspoons grated orange peel (optional)**
1/2 **teaspoon vanilla**
1/2 **cup all-purpose flour**
1/4 **teaspoon salt**
1/3 **cup semisweet chocolate chips**
1/3 **cup coarsely chopped pecans**

1. Heat oven to 375°F. Grease baking sheets with shortening.

2. Combine 1/4 cup shortening, corn syrup, brown sugar, orange peel and vanilla in large bowl. Beat at medium speed of electric mixer until well blended.

3. Combine flour and salt. Mix into creamed mixture at low speed until blended. Stir in chocolate chips and nuts. Drop teaspoonfuls of dough 4 inches apart onto prepared baking sheets.

4. Bake one baking sheet at a time at 375°F for 5 minutes or until edges are golden brown. (Chips and nuts will remain in center while dough spreads out.) *Do not overbake.* Cool 2 minutes on baking sheets. Lift each cookie edge with spatula. Grasp cookie edge gently and lightly pinch or flute the edge, bringing it up to chips and nuts in center. Work around each cookie until completely fluted. Remove to cooling rack. *Makes about 3 dozen cookies*

Crisco.com We cook.

BANANA OATMEAL COOKIES WITH BANANA FROSTING

COOKIES

- ³/₄ Butter Flavor CRISCO® Stick or ³/₄ cup Butter Flavor CRISCO® all-vegetable shortening plus additional for greasing
- 1 cup firmly packed brown sugar
- 1 egg
- 1 cup mashed ripe bananas (2 to 3 medium)
- 1¹/₂ cups all-purpose flour
- 1 teaspoon salt
- 1 teaspoon ground cinnamon
- ¹/₂ teaspoon baking soda
- ¹/₄ teaspoon ground nutmeg
- 1³/₄ cups quick oats (not instant or old-fashioned)
- ¹/₂ cup coarsely chopped walnuts

BANANA FROSTING

- 2 tablespoons Butter Flavor CRISCO® all-vegetable shortening
- ¹/₄ cup mashed ripe banana
- 1 teaspoon lemon juice
- 2 cups confectioners' sugar
  Finely chopped walnuts (optional)

1. Heat oven to 350°F. Grease baking sheets with shortening.

2. For cookies, combine ³/₄ cup shortening and sugar in large bowl. Beat at medium speed of electric mixer until well blended. Beat in egg. Add 1 cup mashed banana. Beat until blended.

3. Combine flour, salt, cinnamon, baking soda and nutmeg in medium bowl. Mix into creamed mixture at low speed until blended. Stir in oats and nuts with spoon.

4. Drop 2 level measuring tablespoonfuls of dough into a mound on prepared baking sheet. Repeat for each cookie, placing about 2 inches apart.

5. Bake at 350°F for 15 to 17 minutes or until set. Cool 1 minute on baking sheet. Remove to cooling rack. Cool completely.

6. For frosting, combine 2 tablespoons shortening, ¹/₄ cup mashed banana and lemon juice in medium bowl. Beat at medium speed of electric mixer until well blended. Add confectioners' sugar, 1 cup at a time. Beat at low speed after each addition until blended. Frost cooled cookies. Sprinkle with nuts, if desired.

Makes about 5 dozen cookies

FROSTED HOLIDAY CUT-OUTS

1¼ cups granulated sugar
1 Butter Flavor CRISCO® Stick
   or 1 cup Butter Flavor
   CRISCO® all-vegetable
   shortening
2 eggs
¼ cup light corn syrup or
   regular pancake syrup
1 tablespoon vanilla
3 cups plus 4 tablespoons
   all-purpose flour, divided
¾ teaspoon baking powder
½ teaspoon baking soda
½ teaspoon salt

ICING

1 cup confectioners' sugar
2 tablespoons milk
   Food color (optional)
   Decorating icing

1. Combine sugar and shortening in large bowl. Beat at medium speed of electric mixer until well blended. Add eggs, syrup and vanilla; beat until well blended and fluffy. Combine 3 cups flour, baking powder, baking soda and salt in medium bowl. Gradually add to shortening mixture, beating at low speed until well blended. Divide dough into 4 equal pieces; shape each into disk. Wrap with plastic wrap. Refrigerate 1 hour or until firm.

2. Heat oven to 375°F. Place sheets of foil on countertop for cooling cookies. Sprinkle about 1 tablespoon flour on large sheet of waxed paper. Place disk of dough on floured paper; flatten slightly with hands. Turn dough over; cover with another large sheet of waxed paper. Roll dough to ¼-inch thickness. Remove top sheet of waxed paper. Cut into desired shapes with floured cookie cutters. Place 2 inches apart on ungreased baking sheet. Repeat with remaining dough.

3. Bake one baking sheet at a time at 375°F for 5 to 7 minutes or until edges of cookies are lightly browned. *Do not overbake.* Cool 2 minutes on baking sheet. Remove cookies to foil to cool completely.

4. For icing, combine confectioners' sugar and milk; stir until smooth. Add food color, if desired. Stir until blended. Spread icing on cookies; place on foil until icing is set. Decorate as desired with decorating icing.
Makes about 3½ dozen cookies

Kitchen Hint. . . . . . .

Before you begin frosting and decorating the cookies, place waxed paper under the wire rack to keep your counters clean and make cleanup easier.

CHERRY CHEESE BARS

BASE
- **1 cup walnut pieces, divided**
- **1¼ cups all-purpose flour**
- **½ cup firmly packed brown sugar**
- **½ Butter Flavor CRISCO® Stick or ½ cup Butter Flavor CRISCO® all-vegetable shortening plus additional for greasing**
- **½ cup flake coconut**

FILLING
- **2 packages (8 ounces each) cream cheese, softened**
- **⅔ cup granulated sugar**
- **2 eggs**
- **2 teaspoons vanilla**
- **1 can (21 ounces) cherry pie filling***

You may substitute another fruit pie filling for the cherry pie filling.

1. Heat oven to 350°F. Grease 13×9×2-inch pan with shortening. Place cooling rack on countertop.

2. Chop ½ cup nuts coarsely. Reserve for topping. Chop remaining ½ cup nuts finely.

3. For base, combine flour and brown sugar in medium bowl. Cut in shortening until fine crumbs form. Add ½ cup finely chopped nuts and coconut. Mix well. Reserve ½ cup crumbs for topping. Press remaining crumbs in bottom of pan. Bake at 350°F for 12 to 15 minutes or until edges are lightly browned. *Do not overbake.*

4. For filling, combine cream cheese, granulated sugar, eggs and vanilla in small bowl. Beat at medium speed of electric mixer until well blended. Spread over hot baked base. Return to oven. Bake for 15 minutes. *Do not overbake.*

5. Spread cherry pie filling over cheese layer.

6. Combine reserved coarsely chopped nuts and reserved crumbs. Sprinkle over pie filling. Return to oven. Bake for 15 minutes. *Do not overbake.* Cool in pan on cooling rack. Refrigerate several hours. Cut into 2×1½-inch bars.

Makes 3 dozen bars

Kitchen Hint. . . . . . .

Store brown sugar in a sealed plastic bag. It stays moist, measures easily and can be packed into a cup through the bag—no more sticky hands.

Cherry Cheese Bars

FROSTY'S COLORFUL COOKIES

1¼ cups firmly packed light
    brown sugar
¾ Butter Flavor CRISCO® Stick
    or ¾ cup Butter Flavor
    CRISCO® all-vegetable
    shortening
2 tablespoons milk
1 tablespoon vanilla
1 egg
1¾ cups all-purpose flour
1 teaspoon salt
¾ teaspoon baking soda
2 cups candy-coated
    chocolate pieces

1. Heat oven to 375°F. Place sheets
of foil on countertop for cooling
cookies.

2. Place brown sugar, shortening,
milk and vanilla in large bowl. Beat
at medium speed of electric mixer
until well blended. Add egg; beat
well.

3. Combine flour, salt and baking
soda. Add to shortening mixture;
beat at low speed just until blended.
Stir in candy-coated chocolate
pieces.

4. Drop dough by rounded
measuring tablespoonfuls 3 inches
apart onto ungreased baking sheets.

5. Bake one baking sheet at a time
at 375°F for 8 to 10 minutes for
chewy cookies, or 11 to 13 minutes
for crisp cookies. *Do not overbake.*
Cool 2 minutes on baking sheet.
Remove cookies to foil to cool
completely.

Makes about 3 dozen cookies

PINEAPPLE COCONUT SNOWBALLS

1 cup sugar
½ Butter Flavor CRISCO® Stick
    or ½ cup Butter Flavor
    CRISCO® all-vegetable
    shortening plus additional
    for greasing
1 egg
½ cup well-drained crushed
    pineapple*
2 cups all-purpose flour
¼ teaspoon salt
¼ teaspoon baking soda
1 can (3½ ounces) flake
    coconut
½ cup coarsely chopped
    pecans

*Place drained pineapple on paper towels.

1. Heat oven to 375°F. Grease
baking sheet with shortening. Place
sheets of foil on countertop for
cooling cookies.

2. Combine sugar and ½ cup
shortening in large bowl. Beat at
medium speed with electric mixer
until well blended. Beat in egg. Mix
in pineapple.

3. Combine flour, salt and baking
soda. Add gradually to creamed
mixture at low speed. Mix until well
blended. Stir in coconut and nuts.
Drop by teaspoonfuls 2 inches apart
onto prepared baking sheet.

4. Bake at 375°F for 10 to
11 minutes. *Do not overbake.* Cool
2 minutes on baking sheet. Remove
cookies to foil to cool completely.

Makes 4 dozen cookies

IRRESISTIBLE PEANUT BUTTER JACK O'LANTERNS

COOKIES

1¼ cups firmly packed light
    brown sugar
¾ cup JIF® Creamy Peanut
    Butter
½ CRISCO® Stick or ½ cup
    CRISCO® all-vegetable
    shortening
3 tablespoons milk
1 tablespoon vanilla
1 egg
1¾ cups all-purpose flour
¾ teaspoon baking soda
¾ teaspoon salt

ICING

1 cup (6 ounces) semisweet
    chocolate chips
2 teaspoons Butter Flavor
    CRISCO® Stick or
2 teaspoons Butter Flavor
    CRISCO® all-vegetable
    shortening

1. Heat oven to 375°F. Place sheets of foil on countertop for cooling cookies.

2. For cookies, place brown sugar, peanut butter, ½ cup shortening, milk and vanilla in large bowl. Beat at medium speed of electric mixer until well blended. Add egg; beat just until blended.

3. Combine flour, baking soda and salt. Add to shortening mixture; beat at low speed just until blended.

4. Pinch off pieces of dough the size of walnuts. Shape into balls. Place 3 inches apart on ungreased baking sheet. Flatten each ball with bottom of glass to approximately ³/₈-inch thickness. Form into pumpkin shape, making indentation on top of round. Pinch off very small piece of dough and roll to form small stem. Attach to top of cookie. Score dough with vertical lines with small, sharp knife to resemble pumpkin.

5. Bake one baking sheet at a time at 375°F for 7 to 8 minutes or until cookies are set and just beginning to brown. *Do not overbake.* Cool on baking sheet 2 minutes. Remove cookies to foil to cool completely.

6. For icing, place chocolate chips and shortening in heavy resealable sandwich bag; seal bag. Microwave at 50% (MEDIUM) for 1 minute. Knead bag. If necessary, microwave at 50% for another 30 seconds at a time until mixture is smooth when bag is kneaded. Cut small tip off corner of bag. Pipe lines and faces on cookies to resemble jack o' lanterns.

Makes about 3 dozen cookies

ST. PAT'S PINWHEELS

1 1/4 cups granulated sugar
1 Butter Flavor CRISCO® Stick
   or 1 cup Butter Flavor
   CRISCO® all-vegetable
   shortening
2 eggs
1/4 cup light corn syrup or
   regular pancake syrup
1 tablespoon vanilla
3 cups all-purpose flour plus
   2 tablespoons, divided
3/4 teaspoon baking powder
1/2 teaspoon baking soda
1/2 teaspoon salt
1/2 teaspoon peppermint
   extract
   Green food color

1. Place sugar and shortening in large bowl. Beat at medium speed of electric mixer until well blended. Add eggs, syrup and vanilla; beat until well blended and fluffy.

2. Combine 3 cups flour, baking powder, baking soda and salt. Add gradually to shortening mixture, beating at low speed until well blended.

3. Place half of dough in medium bowl. Stir in peppermint extract and food color, a few drops at a time, until desired shade of green. Shape each dough into disk. Wrap with plastic wrap. Refrigerate several hours or until firm.

4. Sprinkle about 1 tablespoon flour on large sheet of waxed paper. Place peppermint dough on floured paper; flatten slightly with hands. Turn dough over; cover with another large sheet of waxed paper. Roll dough into 14×9-inch rectangle. Set aside. Repeat with plain dough.

5. Remove top sheet of waxed paper from both doughs. Invert plain dough onto peppermint dough, aligning edges carefully. Remove waxed paper from plain dough. Trim dough to form rectangle. Roll dough tightly in jelly-roll fashion starting with long side and using bottom sheet of waxed paper as guide, removing waxed paper during rolling. Wrap roll in waxed paper; freeze at least 30 minutes or until very firm.

6. Heat oven to 375°F. Place sheets of foil on countertop for cooling cookies.

7. Remove roll from freezer; remove wrapping. Cut roll into 3/8-inch-thick slices. Place slices 2 inches apart on ungreased baking sheet.

8. Bake one baking sheet at a time at 375°F for 7 to 9 minutes or until edges of cookies are very lightly browned. *Do not overbake.* Cool 2 minutes on baking sheet. Remove cookies to foil to cool completely.
Makes about 3 dozen cookies

St. Pat's Pinwheels

HAYSTACKS

¼ **Butter Flavor CRISCO® Stick or ¼ cup Butter Flavor CRISCO® all-vegetable shortening**
½ **cup JIF® Creamy Peanut Butter**
2 **cups butterscotch-flavored chips**
6 **cups corn flakes**
⅔ **cup semisweet miniature chocolate chips**
 Chopped peanuts or chocolate jimmies (optional)

1. Combine shortening, peanut butter and butterscotch chips in large microwave-safe bowl. Cover with waxed paper. Microwave at 50% (MEDIUM). Stir after 1 minute. Repeat until smooth (or melt on rangetop in small saucepan on very low heat, stirring constantly).

2. Pour corn flakes into large bowl. Pour hot butterscotch mixture over flakes. Stir with spoon until flakes are coated. Stir in chocolate chips.

3. Spoon scant ¼ cup mixture into mounds on waxed paper-lined baking sheets. Sprinkle with chopped nuts, if desired. Refrigerate until firm.
Makes about 3 dozen cookies

P.B. GRAHAM SNACKERS

½ **Butter Flavor CRISCO® Stick or ½ cup Butter Flavor CRISCO® all-vegetable shortening**
2 **cups confectioners' sugar**
¾ **cup JIF® Creamy Peanut Butter**
1 **cup graham cracker crumbs**
½ **cup semisweet chocolate chips**
½ **cup graham cracker crumbs or crushed peanuts or colored sugar or sprinkles (optional)**

1. Combine ½ cup shortening, confectioners' sugar and peanut butter in large bowl. Beat at low speed with electric mixer until well blended. Stir in 1 cup crumbs and chocolate chips. Cover and refrigerate 1 hour.

2. Form dough into 1-inch balls. Roll in ½ cup crumbs, peanuts, colored sugar or sprinkles. Cover and refrigerate until ready to serve.
Makes about 3 dozen cookies

Top to bottom: Haystacks and P.B. Graham Snackers

Crisco.com We cook.

PEANUT BUTTER PIZZA COOKIES

1¼ cups firmly packed light
   brown sugar
¾ cup JIF® Creamy Peanut
   Butter
½ CRISCO® Stick or ½ cup
   CRISCO® all-vegetable
   shortening
3 tablespoons milk
1 tablespoon vanilla
1 egg
1¾ cups all-purpose flour
¾ teaspoon salt
¾ teaspoon baking soda
8 ounces white baking
   chocolate, chopped
   Decorative candies

1. Heat oven to 375°F. Place sheets of foil on countertop for cooling cookies.

2. Combine brown sugar, peanut butter, shortening, milk and vanilla in large bowl. Beat at medium speed of electric mixer until well blended. Add egg. Beat just until blended.

3. Combine flour, salt and baking soda. Add to creamed mixture at low speed. Mix just until blended.

4. Divide dough in half. Form each half into a ball. Place 1 ball of dough onto center of ungreased pizza pan or baking sheet. Spread dough with fingers to form a 12-inch circle. Repeat with other ball of dough.

5. Bake one baking sheet at a time at 375°F for 10 to 12 minutes or until lightly browned. *Do not overbake.* Cool 2 minutes on baking sheet. Remove with large spatula to foil to cool completely.

6. Place white chocolate in a shallow microwave-safe bowl. Microwave at 100% (HIGH) for 30 seconds. Stir. Repeat at 30-second intervals until white chocolate is melted.

7. Spread melted white chocolate on center of cooled cookies to within ½ inch of edge. Decorate with candies. Let set completely. Cut into wedges. *Makes 2 pizzas*

Peanut Butter Pizza Cookie

ORANGE PUMPKIN BARS

BARS
- 1½ cups all-purpose flour
- 1 teaspoon baking powder
- 1 teaspoon pumpkin pie spice
- ½ teaspoon baking soda
- ½ teaspoon salt
- 1 cup canned solid-pack pumpkin (not pumpkin pie filling)
- ¾ cup granulated sugar
- ⅔ cup CRISCO® Oil*
- 2 eggs
- ¼ cup firmly packed light brown sugar
- 2 tablespoons orange juice
- ½ cup chopped nuts
- ½ cup raisins

ICING
- 1½ cups confectioners' sugar
- 2 tablespoons orange juice
- 2 tablespoons butter or margarine, softened
- ½ teaspoon grated orange peel

Use your favorite Crisco Oil product.

1. Heat oven to 350°F. Grease and flour 12×8-inch baking pan; set aside. Place wire rack on countertop for cooling bars.

2. For bars, combine flour, baking powder, pumpkin pie spice, baking soda and salt in medium mixing bowl; set aside.

3. Combine pumpkin, granulated sugar, oil, eggs, brown sugar and orange juice in large mixing bowl. Beat at low speed of electric mixer until blended, scraping bowl constantly. Add flour mixture. Beat at medium speed until smooth, scraping bowl frequently. Stir in nuts and raisins. Pour into prepared pan.

4. Bake at 350°F for 35 minutes or until center springs back when touched lightly. *Do not overbake.* Cool bars completely in pan on cooling rack.

5. For icing, combine all ingredients. Beat at medium speed of electric mixer until smooth. Spread over cooled base. Cut into bars.   *Makes about 24 bars*

Yummy Oatmeal Apple Cookie Squares

1 Butter Flavor **CRISCO**® Stick or 1 cup Butter Flavor **CRISCO**® all-vegetable shortening plus additional for greasing
1 cup firmly packed brown sugar
1 cup granulated sugar
2 eggs
$^{1}/_{3}$ cup apple juice
2 teaspoons vanilla
1$^{1}/_{2}$ cups all-purpose flour
2 teaspoons ground cinnamon
1 teaspoon baking powder
1 teaspoon baking soda
$^{1}/_{4}$ teaspoon nutmeg
4 cups quick oats (not instant or old-fashioned)
2 cups peeled, diced apples
$^{1}/_{2}$ cup raisins (optional)

1. Heat oven to 350°F. Grease 15$^{1}/_{2}$×10$^{1}/_{2}$×1-inch pan with shortening.

2. Combine shortening, brown sugar and granulated sugar in large bowl. Beat at medium speed of electric mixer until well blended. Beat in eggs, apple juice and vanilla.

3. Combine flour, cinnamon, baking powder, baking soda and nutmeg. Mix into creamed mixture at low speed until blended. Stir in oats, apples and raisins with spoon. Spread in pan.

4. Bake at 350°F for 30 to 35 minutes or until browned and toothpick inserted in center comes out clean. *Do not overbake.* Cool in pan on cooling rack. Cut into 2$^{1}/_{2}$×1$^{1}/_{2}$-inch bars.

Makes 3$^{1}/_{2}$ dozen bars

Kitchen Hint. . . . . . .

Quick oats and old-fashioned oats are essentially the same. However, the quick oats simply cook faster because they have been rolled into thinner flakes.

Cookies and Bars

LEMON PECAN COOKIES

1 Butter Flavor CRISCO® Stick or 1 cup Butter Flavor CRISCO®
  all-vegetable shortening
1½ cups granulated sugar
2 large eggs
3 tablespoons fresh lemon juice
3 cups all-purpose flour
2 teaspoons baking powder
¼ teaspoon salt
1 cup chopped pecans

1. Heat oven to 350°F.

2. Combine shortening and sugar in large bowl. Beat at medium speed with electric mixer until well blended. Beat in eggs and lemon juice until well blended.

3. Combine flour, baking powder and salt in medium bowl. Add to creamed mixture; mix well. Stir in pecans. Spray cookie sheets lightly with CRISCO® No-Stick Cooking Spray. Drop dough by teaspoonfuls about 2 inches apart onto prepared cookie sheets. Bake at 350°F for 10 to 12 minutes or until lightly browned. Cool on cookie sheets 4 minutes; transfer to cooling rack.

Makes about 6 dozen cookies

Crisco.com We cook.

CINNAMON ROLL COOKIES

CINNAMON MIXTURE
- 4 tablespoons granulated sugar
- 1 tablespoon ground cinnamon

COOKIE DOUGH
- 1 Butter Flavor CRISCO® Stick or 1 cup Butter Flavor CRISCO® all-vegetable shortening
- 1 cup firmly packed light brown sugar
- 2 large eggs
- 1 teaspoon vanilla
- 3 cups all-purpose flour
- 2 teaspoons baking powder
- ½ teaspoon salt
- 1 teaspoon ground cinnamon

1. For cinnamon mixture, combine granulated sugar and 1 tablespoon cinnamon in small bowl; mix well. Set aside.

2. For cookie dough, combine shortening and brown sugar in large bowl. Beat at medium speed with electric mixer until well blended. Beat in eggs and vanilla until well blended.

3. Combine flour, baking powder, salt and 1 teaspoon cinnamon in small bowl. Add to creamed mixture; mix well.

4. Turn dough onto sheet of waxed paper. Spread dough into 9×6-inch rectangle using rubber spatula. Sprinkle with 4 tablespoons cinnamon mixture to within 1 inch from edge. Roll up jelly-roll style into log. Dust log with remaining cinnamon mixture. Wrap tightly in plastic wrap; refrigerate 4 hours or overnight.

5. Heat oven to 350°F. Spray cookie sheets with CRISCO® No-Stick Cooking Spray.

6. Slice dough ¼ inch thick. Place on prepared cookie sheets. Bake at 350°F for 8 minutes or until lightly browned on top. Cool on cookie sheets 4 minutes; transfer to cooling racks.

Makes about 5 dozen cookies

Kitchen Hint. . . . . . .

Be careful when working with this dough. It is a stiff dough and can crack easily when rolling. Roll the dough slowly and smooth any cracks with your finger as you go.

Cinnamon Roll Cookies

Crisco.com We cook.

ALMOND COOKIES

1 CRISCO® Stick or 1 cup
   CRISCO® all-vegetable
   shortening
1 cup granulated sugar
1 large egg, lightly beaten
3 tablespoons almond extract
2¼ cups all-purpose flour
1½ teaspoons baking powder
¼ teaspoon salt
   About 48 whole almonds

1. Combine shortening and sugar in large bowl. Beat at medium speed with electric mixer until well blended. Beat in egg and almond extract until well blended.

2. Combine flour, baking powder and salt in medium bowl. Add to creamed mixture; blend well. Wrap dough in plastic wrap and refrigerate 2 hours.

3. Heat oven to 350°F.

4. Roll rounded tablespoonfuls of dough into balls. Place on ungreased cookie sheets about 2 inches apart; flatten slightly with fingertips. Gently press one almond into center of each.

5. Bake at 350°F for 10 to 12 minutes or until cookies are just done but not brown. Cool on cookie sheet 4 minutes; transfer to cooling racks.

Makes about 4 dozen cookies

ESPRESSO SHORTBREAD BARS

1 Butter Flavor CRISCO® Stick
   or 1 cup Butter Flavor
   CRISCO® all-vegetable
   shortening
½ cup firmly packed light
   brown sugar
1 teaspoon vanilla
1 teaspoon instant coffee
2¼ cups all-purpose flour
¼ teaspoon salt

1. Combine shortening and sugar in large bowl. Beat at medium speed with electric mixer until well blended. Beat in vanilla and instant coffee until instant coffee is dissolved and mixture is fluffy.

2. Combine flour and salt in small bowl. Add to creamed mixture until well blended. Refrigerate dough 4 hours or overnight.

3. Heat oven to 325°F.

4. Spray cookie sheets with CRISCO® No-Stick Cooking Spray. Roll dough out to ¼ inch thick. Cut dough into rectangular bars 3×1 inches long; prick tops with fork and place on prepared cookie sheets. Bake at 325°F for 20 to 25 minutes or until golden. Cool on cookie sheets 4 minutes; transfer to cooling racks.

Makes about 3 dozen bars

Crisco.com We cook.

CHEWY MACADAMIA NUT BLONDIES

3/4 Butter Flavor CRISCO® Stick or 3/4 cup Butter Flavor CRISCO® all-vegetable shortening
1 cup firmly packed light brown sugar
1 large egg
1 teaspoon vanilla
1 teaspoon almond extract
1 cup all-purpose flour
1/2 teaspoon baking soda
1/8 teaspoon salt
6 ounces white chocolate chips
1 cup chopped macadamia nuts

1. Heat oven to 325°F.

2. Combine shortening and sugar in large bowl. Beat at medium speed with electric mixer until well blended. Beat in egg, vanilla and almond extract until well blended.

3. Combine flour, baking soda and salt in small bowl. Add to creamed mixture until just incorporated. *Do not over mix.* Fold in white chocolate chips and nuts until just blended.

4. Spray 9-inch square baking pan with CRISCO® No-Stick Cooking Spray. Pour batter into prepared pan. Bake at 325°F for 25 to 30 minutes or until a wooden pick inserted in center comes out almost dry and top is golden. *Do not over bake or brown.*

5. Place on cooling rack; cool completely. Cut into bars.
Makes about 16 bars

APRICOT ANGEL COOKIES

1 Butter Flavor CRISCO® Stick or 1 cup Butter Flavor CRISCO® all-vegetable shortening
1/2 cup granulated sugar
1/2 cup firmly packed light brown sugar
2 large eggs
1 teaspoon vanilla
2 cups all-purpose flour
1 teaspoon baking soda
1/2 teaspoon salt
2 cups dried apricots, chopped

1. Heat oven to 350°F.

2. Combine shortening and sugars in large bowl. Beat at medium speed with electric mixer until well blended. Beat in eggs and vanilla until well blended.

3. Combine flour, baking soda and salt in medium bowl. Add to creamed mixture; mix well. Mix in apricots. Drop dough by tablespoonfuls onto ungreased cookie sheets about 2 inches apart.

4. Bake at 350°F for 10 to 12 minutes or until edges are lightly browned. Cool on cookie sheets 4 minutes; transfer to cooling racks.
Makes about 4 dozen cookies

APPLE GOLDEN RAISIN CHEESECAKE BARS

1½ **cups rolled oats**
¾ **cup all-purpose flour**
½ **cup firmly packed light brown sugar**
¾ **cup plus 2 tablespoons granulated sugar, divided**
¾ **Butter Flavor CRISCO® Stick or ¾ cup Butter Flavor CRISCO® all-vegetable shortening**
2 **(8-ounce) packages cream cheese, softened**
2 **large eggs**
1 **teaspoon vanilla**
1 **cup chopped Granny Smith apples**
½ **cup golden raisins**
1 **teaspoon almond extract**
½ **teaspoon ground cinnamon**
¼ **teaspoon ground nutmeg**
¼ **teaspoon ground allspice**

1. Heat oven to 350°F.

2. Combine oats, flour, brown sugar and ¼ cup granulated sugar in large bowl; mix well. Cut in shortening with fork until crumbs form. Reserve 1 cup mixture.

3. Spray 13×9-inch baking pan with CRISCO® No-Stick Cooking Spray. Press remaining mixture onto bottom of prepared pan. Bake at 350°F for 12 to 15 minutes or until mixture is set. *Do not brown.* Place on cooling rack.

4. Combine cream cheese, eggs, ½ cup granulated sugar and vanilla in large bowl. Beat at medium speed with electric mixer until well blended. Spread evenly over crust.

5. Combine apples and raisins in medium bowl. Add almond extract; stir. Add remaining 2 tablespoons granulated sugar, cinnamon, nutmeg and allspice; mix well. Top cream cheese mixture evenly with apple mixture; sprinkle reserved oat mixture evenly over top. Bake at 350°F for 20 to 25 minutes or until top is golden. Place on cooling rack; cool completely. Cut into bars.

Makes 18 bars

Kitchen Hint. . . . . . .

Forgot to take the cream cheese out to soften? Don't worry, simply remove it from the wrapper and place it in a medium microwave-safe bowl. Microwave at MEDIUM (50% power) 15 to 20 seconds or until slightly softened.

Apple Golden Raisin Cheesecake Bars

PISTACHIO AND WHITE CHOCOLATE COOKIES

1 cup shelled pistachio nuts
1¼ cups firmly packed light brown sugar
¾ Butter Flavor CRISCO® Stick or ¾ cup Butter Flavor CRISCO® all-vegetable shortening
2 tablespoons milk
1 tablespoon vanilla
1 egg
1¾ cups all-purpose flour
1 teaspoon salt
¾ teaspoon baking soda
1 cup white chocolate chips or chunks

1. Heat oven to 350°F. Spread pistachio nuts on baking sheet. Bake at 350°F for 7 to 10 minutes or until toasted, stirring several times. Place nuts in kitchen towel; rub with towel to remove most of skin. Cool nuts. Chop coarsely; reserve.

2. Increase oven temperature to 375°F. Place sheets of foil on countertop for cooling cookies.

3. Place brown sugar, shortening, milk and vanilla in large bowl. Beat at medium speed with electric mixer until well blended. Add egg; beat well.

4. Combine flour, salt and baking soda in medium bowl. Add to shortening mixture; beat at low speed just until blended. Stir in white chocolate chips and reserved pistachios.

5. Drop by rounded tablespoonfuls of dough 3 inches apart onto ungreased cookie sheets.

6. Bake one baking sheet at a time at 375°F for 8 to 10 minutes for chewy cookies, or 11 to 13 minutes for crisp cookies. *Do not overbake.* Cool 2 minutes on cookie sheet. Remove to foil to cool completely.
Makes about 3 dozen cookies

RASPBERRY CRISP BARS

CRUST
½ Butter Flavor CRISCO® Stick or ½ cup Butter Flavor CRISCO® all-vegetable shortening
⅓ cup confectioners' sugar
1 cup all-purpose flour

TOPPING
½ cup all-purpose flour
3 tablespoons firmly packed light brown sugar
¼ teaspoon baking powder
¼ teaspoon ground cinnamon
4 tablespoons Butter Flavor CRISCO® all-vegetable shortening
1 egg yolk
½ teaspoon vanilla
¾ cup SMUCKER'S® Raspberry Preserves or any flavor

1. Heat oven to 350°F.

2. For crust, combine shortening and confectioners' sugar in large bowl. Beat at medium speed with electric mixer until well blended. Stir in 1 cup flour until mixture is just crumbly. Press onto bottom of ungreased 8-inch square baking pan. Bake at 350°F for 10 to 12 minutes or until crust is set but not browned. Remove from oven and place on cooling rack.

3. For topping, combine ½ cup flour, brown sugar, baking powder and cinnamon in medium bowl; mix well. Cut in shortening with fork until mixture forms even crumbs. Add egg yolk and vanilla; mix well.

4. Spread preserves evenly over crust. Sprinkle topping evenly over preserves. Bake at 350°F for 30 minutes or until topping is golden. Place on cooling rack and allow to cool completely. Cut into bars.   *Makes 1 dozen bars*

CHOCOLATE CHIP ALMOND OATMEAL COOKIES

- 1 Butter Flavor CRISCO® Stick or 1 cup Butter Flavor CRISCO® all-vegetable shortening
- 1 cup granulated sugar
- 1 cup firmly packed dark brown sugar
- 2 large eggs
- 1 teaspoon vanilla
- ½ teaspoon almond extract
- 2 cups all-purpose flour
- 1 teaspoon baking soda
- ½ teaspoon salt
- 2 cups rolled oats
- 9 ounces semisweet chocolate chips
- 1 cup slivered almonds

1. Heat oven to 350°F.

2. Combine shortening and sugars in large bowl. Beat at medium speed with electric mixer until well blended. Beat in eggs, vanilla and almond extract until well blended.

3. Combine flour, baking soda and salt in medium bowl. Add to creamed mixture; mix well. Add oats; mix well. Add chocolate chips and almonds.

4. Spray cookie sheets with CRISCO® No-Stick Cooking Spray. Drop dough by tablespoonfuls 2 inches apart onto prepared cookie sheets. Bake at 350°F for 10 to 12 minutes or until lightly browned. Cool on cookie sheets 4 minutes; transfer to cooling racks.

Makes about 4 dozen cookies

PEANUT BUTTER AND JELLY COOKIES

1 Butter Flavor CRISCO® Stick
   or 1 cup Butter Flavor
   CRISCO® all-vegetable
   shortening
1 cup JIF® Creamy Peanut
   Butter
1 teaspoon vanilla
²/₃ cup firmly packed light
   brown sugar
¹/₃ cup granulated sugar
2 large eggs
2 cups all-purpose flour
1 cup SMUCKER'S® Strawberry
   Preserves or any flavor

1. Heat oven to 350°F.

2. Combine shortening, peanut butter and vanilla in food processor fitted with metal blade. Process until well blended and smooth. Add sugars; process until incorporated completely. Add eggs, process just until blended. Add flour; pulse until dough begins to form ball. *Do not over process.*

3. Place dough in medium bowl. Shape ¹/₂ tablespoon dough into ball for each cookie. Place 1¹/₂ inches apart on ungreased cookie sheets. Press thumb into center of each ball to create deep well. Fill each well with about ¹/₂ teaspoon preserves.

4. Bake at 350°F for 10 minutes or until lightly browned and firm. Cool on cookie sheets 4 minutes; transfer to cooling racks. Leave on racks about 30 minutes or until completely cool.

Makes about 5 dozen cookies

CITRUS–GINGER COOKIES

1 Butter Flavor CRISCO® Stick
   or 1 cup Butter Flavor
   CRISCO® all-vegetable
   shortening
1¹/₂ cups granulated sugar
1 large egg
2 tablespoons light corn syrup
1 teaspoon vanilla
3 cups all-purpose flour
1 tablespoon ground ginger
2 teaspoons baking soda
¹/₂ teaspoon fresh grated
   orange peel
¹/₂ teaspoon fresh grated
   lemon peel
¹/₂ teaspoon fresh grated lime
   peel

1. Combine shortening and sugar in large bowl. Beat at medium speed with electric mixer until well blended. Beat in egg, corn syrup and vanilla until well blended.

2. Combine flour, ginger and baking soda in small bowl. Add to creamed mixture. Add orange, lemon and lime peel until well blended.

3. Shape dough into two rolls about 2 inches in diameter. Wrap tightly in plastic wrap; refrigerate 3 hours or overnight.

4. Heat oven to 350°F.

5. Slice dough about ¹/₈ inch thick. Place slices 2 inches apart on ungreased cookie sheets. Bake at 350°F for 6 to 8 minutes or until lightly brown. Cool on cookie sheets 4 minutes; transfer to cooling racks.

Makes about 7 dozen cookies

Peanut Butter and Jelly Cookies

Crisco.com We cook.

COCONUT CREAM CHEESE COOKIES

1 Butter Flavor CRISCO® Stick or 1 cup Butter Flavor CRISCO® all-vegetable shortening
6 ounces cream cheese, softened
1 cup granulated sugar
1 teaspoon almond extract
1 teaspoon vanilla
1/4 teaspoon salt
1 large egg
2 tablespoons milk
2 cups all-purpose flour
1/2 cup toasted flaked coconut

1. Heat oven to 325°F.

2. Combine shortening, cream cheese, sugar, almond extract, vanilla and salt in large bowl. Beat at medium speed with electric mixer until well blended. Beat in egg and milk until well blended. Add flour and coconut; mix well.

3. Drop rounded teaspoonfuls of dough about 2 inches apart onto ungreased cookie sheets.

4. Bake at 325°F for 15 to 20 minutes or until lightly browned. Cool on cookie sheets 4 minutes; transfer to cooling racks.
Makes about 5 dozen cookies

CHEF'S "MIDNIGHT SNACK" CHOCOLATE CHIP COOKIES

1 CRISCO® Stick or 1 cup CRISCO® all-vegetable shortening
1 cup granulated sugar
1/2 cup light brown sugar
2 large eggs
2 teaspoons vanilla
1/2 teaspoon baking powder
1/4 teaspoon salt
2 1/4 cups cake flour
1 pound chocolate chips

1. Combine shortening and sugars in large bowl. Beat on medium speed with electric mixer until well blended. Beat in eggs, vanilla, baking powder and salt until well blended. Stir in cake flour.

2. Stir in chocolate chips just until mixed in. Shape dough into two rolls about 2 inches in diameter. Wrap tightly in plastic and refrigerate 4 hours or overnight.

3. Heat oven to 350°F.

4. Slice dough about 1/2 inch thick. Place slices on ungreased cookie sheets. Bake at 350°F for 10 to 14 minutes or until firm and golden. Cool on cookie sheets 4 minutes; transfer to cooling racks.
Makes about 4 dozen cookies

Coconut Cream Cheese Cookies

Crisco.com **We cook.**

SUN DRIED CRANBERRY–WALNUT OATMEAL COOKIES

¾ Butter Flavor CRISCO® Stick or ¾ cup Butter Flavor CRISCO® all-vegetable shortening
¾ cup granulated sugar
¾ cup firmly packed light brown sugar
2 large eggs
1 teaspoon vanilla
1 cup all-purpose flour
1 teaspoon baking soda
¼ teaspoon salt
2¾ cups rolled oats
1 cup sun dried cranberries
1 cup walnut pieces

1. Heat oven to 375°F.

2. Combine shortening and sugars in large bowl. Beat at medium speed with electric mixer until well blended. Beat in eggs and vanilla until well blended.

3. Combine flour, baking soda and salt in small bowl. Stir into creamed mixture; mix well. Add oats, sun dried cranberries and walnuts. Spray cookie sheets with CRISCO® No-Stick Cooking Spray. Dust with flour. Drop dough by teaspoonfuls about 2 inches apart onto prepared cookie sheets. Bake at 375°F for 8 minutes or until firm and brown. Cool on cookie sheets 4 minutes; transfer to cooling rack.

Makes about 6 dozen cookies

BUTTERSCOTCH OAT BARS

1¾ cups rolled oats
1½ cups all-purpose flour
¾ cup firmly packed light brown sugar
½ teaspoon baking soda
½ teaspoon salt
¾ cup CRISCO® Canola Oil
1 teaspoon vanilla
11 ounces butterscotch-flavored chips

1. Heat oven to 350°F.

2. Combine oats, flour, sugar, baking soda and salt in large bowl; mix well. Add oil and vanilla; mix until well combined and crumbly. Add butterscotch chips; mix evenly.

3. Spray 8-inch square baking pan with CRISCO® No-Stick Cooking Spray. Lightly press mixture into baking pan. Bake at 350°F for 17 to 20 minutes or until top is golden. Cool completely on cooling rack. Cut into bars.   *Makes about 16 bars*

Sun Dried Cranberry– Walnut Oatmeal Cookies

Crisco.com We cook.

Cakes and Sweet Breads

SUN DRIED CHERRY–ORANGE COFFEE CAKE

 2 cups all-purpose flour
1/2 cup granulated sugar
 3 teaspoons baking powder
1/2 teaspoon salt
1/2 cup CRISCO® Canola Oil
1/2 cup milk
 1 egg, beaten
1/2 cup chopped sun dried cherries
1/2 cup fresh orange juice
 2 teaspoons grated fresh orange peel
1/2 cup packed light brown sugar
1/2 cup chopped pecans
 2 tablespoons butter, softened
 1 teaspoon ground cinnamon
1/2 teaspoon ground nutmeg

1. Heat oven to 375°F. Sift together flour, sugar, baking powder and salt in large bowl. Combine oil, milk and egg in small bowl; mix well. Add to flour mixture; stir until blended. Combine cherries, orange juice and orange peel in large bowl; mix well. Add to batter until blended.

2. Spray 9-inch square baking pan with CRISCO® No-Stick Cooking Spray. Dust pan with flour. Pour batter into pan; spread evenly. Combine brown sugar, pecans, butter, cinnamon and nutmeg in large bowl; mix well. Sprinkle over batter.

3. Bake at 375°F for 25 to 30 minutes or until toothpick inserted in center comes out clean. Remove from oven and let rest 5 minutes before serving.

Makes 6 to 8 servings

Crisco.com We cook.

COCONUT POUND CAKE

CAKE

- 2 cups granulated sugar
- 1 Butter Flavor CRISCO® Stick or 1 cup Butter Flavor CRISCO® all-vegetable shortening plus additional for greasing
- 5 eggs
- 1½ teaspoons coconut extract
- 2¼ cups all-purpose flour
- 1½ teaspoons baking powder
- ½ teaspoon salt
- 1 cup buttermilk or sour milk*
- 1 cup shredded coconut, chopped

GLAZE

- ½ cup granulated sugar
- ¼ cup water
- 1½ teaspoons coconut extract

GARNISH (OPTIONAL)

**Whipped topping or whipped cream
Assorted fresh fruit**

To sour milk: Combine 1 tablespoon white vinegar plus enough milk to equal 1 cup. Stir. Wait 5 minutes before using.

1. Heat oven to 350°F. Grease 10-inch tube pan with shortening. Flour lightly. Place cooling rack on countertop to cool cake.

2. For cake, combine 2 cups sugar and 1 cup shortening in large bowl. Beat at medium speed of electric mixer until blended. Add eggs, 1 at a time, beating slightly after each addition. Beat in 1½ teaspoons coconut extract.

3. Combine flour, baking powder and salt in medium bowl. Add alternately with buttermilk to creamed mixture, beating at low speed after each addition until well blended. Add coconut. Mix until blended. Spoon into pan.

4. Bake at 350°F for 50 minutes or until toothpick inserted in center comes out clean. *Do not overbake.* Remove to wire rack. Cool for 5 minutes. Remove cake from pan. Place cake, top side up, on serving plate. Use toothpick to poke 12 to 15 holes in top of cake.

5. For glaze, combine ½ cup sugar, water and 1½ teaspoons coconut extract in small saucepan. Cook and stir over medium heat until mixture comes to a boil. Remove from heat. Cool 15 minutes. Spoon over cake. Cool completely.

6. For optional garnish, place spoonfuls of whipped topping and assorted fresh fruit on each serving.

*Makes one 10-inch tube cake
(12 to 16 servings)*

Coconut Pound Cake

CAROL'S CAPPUCCINO CAKE

CAKE
2¼ cups all-purpose flour
2 cups granulated sugar
1 tablespoon plus
    1½ teaspoons instant
    espresso coffee granules
1½ teaspoons baking powder
1½ teaspoons ground
    cinnamon
1 teaspoon baking soda
1 teaspoon salt
1 cup water
¾ cup plus 1 tablespoon dairy
    sour cream
¼ CRISCO® Stick or ¼ cup
    CRISCO® all-vegetable
    shortening plus additional
    for greasing
1 teaspoon vanilla
2 eggs
4 squares (1 ounce each)
    unsweetened baking
    chocolate, melted

FROSTING
2 packages (3 ounces each)
    cream cheese, softened
¾ Butter Flavor CRISCO® Stick
    or ¾ cup Butter Flavor
    CRISCO® all-vegetable
    shortening
4½ cups confectioners' sugar
¼ cup milk
1 tablespoon plus
    1½ teaspoons instant
    espresso coffee granules
1 teaspoon ground cinnamon
1 teaspoon vanilla
4 squares (1 ounce each)
    unsweetened baking
    chocolate, melted

1. Heat oven to 350°F. Grease 13×9×2-inch glass baking dish. Line bottom with waxed paper. Grease waxed paper.

2. For cake, combine flour, granulated sugar, 1 tablespoon plus 1½ teaspoons coffee granules, baking powder, 1½ teaspoons cinnamon, baking soda and salt in large bowl. Add water, sour cream, ¼ cup shortening and 1 teaspoon vanilla. Beat at low speed with electric mixer 1 minute. Add eggs and 4 squares melted chocolate. Beat at medium speed 2 minutes. Pour into prepared dish.

3. Bake at 350°F for 25 to 35 minutes or until toothpick inserted in center comes out clean. *Do not overbake.* Cool 10 minutes before removing from dish. Invert cake onto cooling rack. Remove waxed paper. Cool completely. Place cake on serving tray.

4. For frosting, beat cream cheese and ¾ cup shortening in large bowl at low speed until blended. Add confectioners' sugar, milk, 1 tablespoon plus 1½ teaspoons coffee granules, 1 teaspoon cinnamon and 1 teaspoon vanilla. Beat until blended. Add 4 squares melted chocolate. Beat at high speed 2 minutes. Frost top and sides of cake. Refrigerate leftover frosting. Serve immediately or refrigerate until serving time. Refrigerate leftovers.
Makes one 13×9 ×2-inch cake
(12 to 16 servings)

Crisco.com We cook.

CRANBERRY APPLE MUFFINS

1/4 Butter Flavor CRISCO® Stick or 1/4 cup Butter Flavor CRISCO® all-vegetable shortening plus additional for greasing
1/2 cup firmly packed brown sugar
2 eggs
1 3/4 cups all-purpose flour
2 teaspoons baking powder
1 teaspoon ground cinnamon
1/2 teaspoon salt
1 cup milk
1 cup peeled and finely chopped fresh apple
1 cup fresh cranberries, rinsed

1. Heat oven to 425°F. Grease muffin pans with shortening or use paper baking cups.

2. Combine shortening, brown sugar and eggs in large bowl. Beat at medium speed with electric mixer until creamy.

3. Combine flour, baking powder, cinnamon and salt in small bowl. Stir until completely mixed. Add to creamed mixture. Add milk, apple and cranberries. Stir just until blended.

4. Spoon batter into muffin cups to three-quarters full.

5. Bake one pan at a time at 425°F for 15 minutes or until toothpick inserted in center comes out clean. *Do not overbake.* Cool 2 minutes in muffin pan. Serve warm.

Makes about 24 muffins

APRICOT NUT BREAD

1 1/2 cups coarsely chopped dried apricots
1 cup water
2 1/2 cups all-purpose flour
3/4 cup granulated sugar
4 teaspoons baking powder
1 teaspoon salt
1/2 teaspoon baking soda
2/3 cup chopped nuts
1 egg, slightly beaten
1 cup buttermilk
3 tablespoons CRISCO® Stick or 3 tablespoons CRISCO® all-vegetable shortening, melted, plus additional for greasing

1. Heat oven to 350°F. Grease bottom of 9×5×3-inch loaf pan.

2. Combine apricots and water in heavy saucepan. Bring to a boil; reduce heat and simmer, uncovered, for 10 minutes or until water is absorbed. Cool.

3. Combine flour, sugar, baking powder, salt and baking soda in large bowl. Stir in nuts.

4. Combine apricots, egg, buttermilk and shortening in medium bowl. Add to dry ingredients. Stir just until dry ingredients are moistened.

5. Spoon batter into prepared pan.

6. Bake at 350°F for 55 to 60 minutes or until toothpick inserted in center comes out clean.

7. Cool for 10 minutes in pan on cooling rack. Remove from pan; cool completely before slicing.

Makes 1 loaf

GLAZED CHOCOLATE POUND CAKE

CAKE

- 1¾ Butter Flavor CRISCO® Stick or 1¾ cups Butter Flavor CRISCO® all-vegetable shortening plus additional for greasing
- 3 cups granulated sugar
- 5 eggs
- 1 teaspoon vanilla
- 3¼ cups all-purpose flour
- ½ cup unsweetened cocoa powder
- 1 teaspoon baking powder
- ½ teaspoon salt
- 1⅓ cups milk
- 1 cup miniature semisweet chocolate chips

GLAZE

- 1 cup miniature semisweet chocolate chips
- ¼ Butter Flavor CRISCO® Stick or ¼ cup Butter Flavor CRISCO® all-vegetable shortening
- 1 tablespoon light corn syrup

1. For cake, heat oven to 325°F. Grease and flour 10-inch tube pan.

2. Combine 1¾ cups shortening, sugar, eggs and vanilla in large bowl. Beat at low speed with electric mixer until blended, scraping bowl constantly. Beat at high speed 6 minutes, scraping bowl occasionally. Combine flour, cocoa, baking powder and salt in medium bowl. Mix in dry ingredients alternately with milk, beating after each addition until batter is smooth. Stir in 1 cup chocolate chips. Spoon into prepared pan.

3. Bake at 325°F for 75 to 85 minutes or until wooden pick inserted in center comes out clean. Cool on cooling rack 20 minutes. Invert onto serving dish. Cool completely.

4. For glaze, combine 1 cup chocolate chips, ¼ cup shortening and corn syrup in top part of double boiler over hot, not boiling water. Stir until just melted and smooth. Cool slightly. (Or place mixture in microwave-safe bowl. Microwave at Medium (50% power) for 1 minute and 15 seconds. Stir. Repeat at 15-second intervals, if necessary, until just melted and smooth. Cool slightly.) Spoon over cake. Let stand until glaze is firm.

Makes 1 (10-inch) tube cake

Glazed Chocolate Pound Cake

APPLE SAUCY OATMEAL–RAISIN LOAF

BREAD

- ½ cup firmly packed brown sugar
- ⅓ cup CRISCO® Oil*
- 4 egg whites
- 1 cup chunky applesauce
- 2 tablespoons water
- 1½ cups quick or old-fashioned oats (not instant), uncooked
- 1¼ cups all-purpose flour
- 1½ teaspoons ground cinnamon
- 1 teaspoon baking powder
- 1 teaspoon baking soda
- ¼ teaspoon salt (optional)
- 1 cup raisins

TOPPING

- 2 tablespoons quick or old-fashioned oats, uncooked
- 1 tablespoon chopped natural almonds
- 1½ teaspoons brown sugar
- ¼ teaspoon ground cinnamon

GARNISH

Applesauce

Use your favorite Crisco Oil product.

1. Heat oven to 375°F. Grease 9×5×3-inch loaf pan.** Place cooling rack on countertop.

2. Combine brown sugar, oil, egg whites, applesauce and water in large bowl.

3. Combine oats, flour, cinnamon, baking powder, baking soda and salt in medium bowl. Stir into liquid ingredients until just blended. Stir in raisins. Spoon into prepared pan.

4. For topping, combine oats, almonds, brown sugar and cinnamon. Sprinkle over top of loaf.

5. Bake at 375°F for 50 to 60 minutes or until golden brown and toothpick inserted in center comes out clean. *Do not overbake.* Cool 10 minutes in pan on cooling rack. Loosen from sides. Remove from pan. Cool completely on cooling rack.

6. To serve, place slice on serving plate. Spoon about 2 tablespoons additional applesauce over top of each slice.

Makes 1 loaf (12 servings)

**For muffins, heat oven to 400°F. Line 12 medium (about 2½-inch) muffin cups with foil or paper liners. Fill muffin cups almost full. Sprinkle with topping. Bake at 400°F for 18 to 22 minutes or until golden brown and toothpick inserted in center comes out clean. Cool 5 minutes before removing from pan. Spoon remaining applesauce over muffin halves, if desired.

Crisco.com **We cook.**

FROSTED ORANGE CHIFFON CAKE

CAKE
- 2 egg whites
- 1 1/3 cups granulated sugar, divided
- 1 3/4 cups cake flour
- 1 tablespoon baking powder
- 1 teaspoon salt
- 1 teaspoon grated orange peel
- 1/2 cup orange juice
- 1/2 cup milk
- 1/2 cup CRISCO® Oil*
- 2 egg yolks

FROSTING
- 4 cups confectioners' sugar
- 1/4 Butter Flavor CRISCO® Stick or 1/4 cup Butter Flavor CRISCO® all-vegetable shortening
- 1/2 teaspoon grated orange peel
- 1/3 cup orange juice

Use your favorite Crisco Oil product.

1. For cake, heat oven to 350°F. Grease and flour two 8-inch round cake pans.

2. Beat egg whites with 1/3 cup granulated sugar in small bowl until thick and glossy but not stiff; set aside. Combine flour, remaining 1 cup granulated sugar, baking powder and salt in large bowl. Add 1 teaspoon orange peel, 1/2 cup orange juice, milk, oil and egg yolks. Mix at medium speed 4 minutes, scraping bottom and sides of bowl often. Fold egg whites into batter until well blended. Pour into pans.

3. Bake at 350°F for 25 to 30 minutes or until center springs back when lightly touched and toothpick inserted in center comes out clean. Cool 10 to 20 minutes. Remove from pans. Cool completely.

4. For frosting, combine confectioners' sugar, shortening and 1/2 teaspoon orange peel in medium bowl. Gradually add 1/3 cup orange juice, beating until smooth and of desired consistency. Spread between layers and over top and sides of cake.

Makes 12 to 16 servings

Kitchen Hint. . . . . .

When grating orange peel, grate only the outer orange layer of the skin, which is very sweet and flavorful. Avoid grating into the white pith, as it is bitter tasting.

PUMPKIN CAKE WITH ORANGE GLAZE

CAKE

2 cups firmly packed light
   brown sugar
¾ Butter Flavor CRISCO® Stick
   or ¾ cup Butter Flavor
   CRISCO® all-vegetable
   shortening plus additional
   for greasing
4 eggs
1 can (16 ounces) solid-pack
   pumpkin (not pumpkin
   pie filling)
¼ cup water
2½ cups cake flour
1 tablespoon plus 1 teaspoon
   baking powder
1 tablespoon pumpkin pie
   spice
1½ teaspoons baking soda
1 teaspoon salt
½ cup chopped walnuts
½ cup raisins

GLAZE

1 cup confectioners' sugar
¾ teaspoon grated orange
   peel
1 tablespoon plus 1 teaspoon
   orange juice
Additional chopped walnuts

1. Heat oven to 350°F. Grease
10-inch (12-cup) Bundt pan. Flour
lightly.

2. For cake, combine brown sugar
and ¾ cup shortening in large bowl.
Beat at low speed with electric mixer
until creamy. Add eggs, 1 at a time,
beating well after each addition. Stir
in pumpkin and water.

3. Combine cake flour, baking
powder, pumpkin pie spice, baking
soda and salt in medium bowl. Add
to pumpkin mixture. Beat at low
speed with electric mixer until
blended. Beat 2 minutes at medium
speed. Fold in ½ cup nuts and
raisins. Spoon into prepared pan.

4. Bake at 350°F for 55 to
60 minutes or until wooden pick
inserted in center comes out clean.
Cool 10 minutes before removing
from pan. Place cake, fluted side up,
on serving plate. Cool completely.

5. For glaze, combine confectioners'
sugar, orange peel and orange juice
in small bowl. Stir with spoon to
blend. Spoon over top of cake,
letting excess glaze run down side.
Sprinkle with additional nuts before
glaze hardens.

*Makes one 10-inch bundt cake
(12 to 16 servings)*

Pumpkin Cake with Orange Glaze

ARLINGTON APPLE GINGERBREAD CAKE

CAKE
- 2 cans (20 ounces each) sliced apples, drained*
- 1 cup plus 1 teaspoon granulated sugar, divided
- 2 teaspoons ground cinnamon, divided
- 2 teaspoons fresh lemon juice
- 1 teaspoon grated lemon peel
- ½ Butter Flavor CRISCO® Stick or ½ cup Butter Flavor CRISCO® all-vegetable shortening
- 1 cup light molasses
- 2 eggs
- 3 cups all-purpose flour
- 2 teaspoons ground ginger
- ½ teaspoon ground cloves
- 1 cup boiling water
- 2 teaspoons baking soda

TOPPING (OPTIONAL)
Confectioners' sugar
Prepared lemon pie filling
Whipped cream

Substitute 4½ cups sliced, peeled, translucent Ida Red or Jonathan apples (about 1½ pounds or 4 to 5 medium apples) for canned if desired. Combine with blended sugar and cinnamon, lemon juice and lemon peel in saucepan. Cook and stir until apples become softened. Transfer mixture to baking pan. Continue as directed in step 3.

1. Heat oven to 350°F.

2. For cake, arrange apple slices in bottom of ungreased 13×9×2-inch baking pan. Combine 1 teaspoon granulated sugar and 1 teaspoon cinnamon in small bowl. Sprinkle over apples along with lemon juice and lemon peel.

3. Combine shortening and remaining 1 cup granulated sugar in large bowl. Beat with spoon until blended. Add molasses and eggs. Beat until blended.

4. Combine flour, ginger, remaining 1 teaspoon cinnamon and cloves in medium bowl. Add to molasses mixture. Beat until blended.

5. Combine boiling water and baking soda. Stir into molasses mixture until blended. Pour over apple mixture.

6. Bake at 350°F for 50 to 60 minutes or until wooden pick inserted in center comes out clean. *Do not overbake.* Cool completely in pan on wire rack.

7. For optional topping, sprinkle top of cake with confectioners' sugar. Place spoonfuls of pie filling and whipped cream on each serving.
Makes one 13×9×2-inch cake (12 to 16 servings)

Crisco.com **We cook.**

BLUEBERRY ORANGE MUFFINS

1/4 **CRISCO® Stick or** 1/4 **cup CRISCO® all-vegetable shortening**
1/3 **cup firmly packed brown sugar**
2 **egg whites, lightly beaten**
2/3 **cup skim milk**
1/3 **cup orange juice**
2 **teaspoons grated orange peel**
1 1/3 **cups all-purpose flour**
1 **cup uncooked old-fashioned or quick oats**
1 **tablespoon baking powder**
1/2 **teaspoon baking soda**
1/2 **teaspoon ground cinnamon**
1/2 **teaspoon salt (optional)**
3/4 **cup fresh or frozen blueberries**

1. Heat oven to 400°F. Line 12 medium (about 2 1/2-inches) muffin cups with foil or paper liners.

2. Combine shortening and brown sugar in large bowl. Beat at medium speed with electric mixer or stir with fork until well blended. Gradually stir in egg whites, milk, orange juice and orange peel.

3. Combine flour, oats, baking powder, baking soda, cinnamon and salt in medium bowl. Stir into liquid ingredients until just blended. Fold in blueberries. Fill muffin cups 2/3 full.

4. Bake at 400°F for 18 to 20 minutes or until golden brown. Serve warm.

Makes 1 dozen muffins

Variation: Substitute 3/4 cup fresh or frozen cranberries, coarsely chopped, for blueberries.

Note: Baked muffins can be frozen. To reheat, microwave at HIGH about 30 seconds per muffin.

Kitchen Hint. . . . . .

Don't overbeat the batter when making muffins. The batter should be lumpy; the lumps will disappear during baking. Overbeating the batter will result in tunnels, peaked tops and a tough texture.

CHOCOLATE CHIP, PEAR AND PISTACHIO LOAF CAKE WITH MOCHA SAUCE

3/4 **Butter Flavor CRISCO® Stick or 3/4 cup Butter Flavor CRISCO® all-vegetable shortening**
1 1/2 **cups all-purpose flour**
3/4 **cup granulated sugar**
3 **eggs**
1 **teaspoon baking powder**
1 **teaspoon vanilla**
1/8 **teaspoon salt**
1 **cup dark chocolate chips**
3/4 **cup shelled unsalted pistachio nuts**
1 **firm ripe pear, peeled, cored and diced small**
Mocha Sauce (recipe follows)

1. Heat oven to 350°F. Combine shortening, flour, sugar, eggs, baking powder, vanilla and salt in food processor. Process about 45 to 60 seconds or until just combined. *Do not over process.* Pour batter into large bowl. Stir in chocolate chips, pistachio nuts and diced pear until ingredients are evenly distributed.

2. Spray 6-cup loaf pan with CRISCO® No-Stick Cooking Spray. Dust pan with flour. Pour batter into prepared pan.

3. Bake at 350°F for 50 to 60 minutes or until toothpick inserted in center comes out clean. Cool 7 to 10 minutes in pan. Turn out onto cooling rack; cool completely. Place one slice of cake on each plate. Drizzle with sauce. Garnish with a slice of fresh pear and pistachio nuts.

Makes 6 to 8 servings

MOCHA SAUCE

8 **ounces dark chocolate finely chopped, room temperature**
1 **cup heavy cream**
1/2 **cup strong brewed coffee (leftover works well)**
1 **teaspoon vanilla**

1. Place chocolate in large heat proof bowl. Combine heavy cream and coffee in small saucepan. Bring to a boil over medium-high heat. Pour over chocolate; gently whisk until chocolate is completely melted and sauce is smooth. Whisk in vanilla. Sauce can be made up to 1 week in advance and stored in refrigerator. Warm gently and whisk well before serving.

Chocolate Chip, Pear and Pistachio Loaf Cake with Mocha Sauce

Crisco.com We cook.

TROPICAL CARROT BREAD

BREAD

- ⅓ **CRISCO® Stick or ⅓ cup CRISCO® all-vegetable shortening plus additional for greasing**
- ¾ **cup firmly packed brown sugar**
- 4 **egg whites, slightly beaten**
- 2¼ **cups all-purpose flour**
- 1 **tablespoon plus 2 teaspoons baking powder**
- ¾ **teaspoon ground cinnamon**
- ¼ **teaspoon ground ginger**
- ¼ **teaspoon salt (optional)**
- 1¼ **cups uncooked old-fashioned or quick oats**
- 1 **cup shredded carrots**
- 1 **can (8 ounces) crushed pineapple in unsweetened juice**
- ½ **cup raisins**

TOPPING

- 2 **tablespoons uncooked old-fashioned or quick oats**

1. Heat oven to 350°F. Grease 9×5×3-inch loaf pan.

2. For bread, combine shortening and brown sugar in large bowl. Beat at medium speed with electric mixer or stir with fork until well blended. Stir in egg whites. Beat until fairly smooth.

3. Combine flour, baking powder, cinnamon, ginger and salt in medium bowl. Stir into egg mixture. Stir in oats. Add carrots and pineapple with juice. Stir until just blended. Stir in raisins. Spoon into prepared pan.

4. For topping, sprinkle oats evenly over top.

5. Bake at 350°F for 70 to 80 minutes or until wooden pick inserted in center comes out clean. Cool 10 minutes in pan on cooling rack. Loosen from sides. Remove from pan. Cool completely on cooling rack.

Makes 1 loaf (12 servings)

Kitchen Hint. . . . . . .

A loaf of homemade bread makes a great gift—especially when it's given in a new loaf pan. Just add a wooden spoon and the recipe, wrap it all up in a festive towel and tie it with ribbon.

Tropical Carrot Bread

Pies and Cobblers

MACADAMIA NUT PIE

1 unbaked Classic CRISCO® Single Crust (page 70)
½ cup butter
½ cup firmly packed light brown sugar
½ teaspoon vanilla
1 pinch salt
¾ cup light corn syrup
3 eggs, beaten
⅔ cup macadamia nuts, coarsely chopped

1. Heat oven to 400°F. Combine butter, brown sugar, vanilla and salt in large bowl until well blended. Slowly stir in corn syrup and eggs; mix well. Fold in nuts and pour into pie crust.

2. Bake at 400°F for 10 minutes. *Reduce oven temperature to 350°F.* Continue to bake at 350°F for an additional 45 minutes or until center is set and firm. Cool to room temperature and serve with whipped cream or ice cream, if desired. *Makes 1 (9-inch) pie (8 servings)*

Crisco.com We cook.

RASPBERRY AND CREAM PIE

CRUST
  1 unbaked Classic CRISCO®
    Single Crust (page 70)

RASPBERRY LAYER
  ³/₄ cup granulated sugar
  ¹/₄ cup cornstarch
  ¹/₈ teaspoon salt
  1³/₄ cups water
  1 package (3 ounces)
    raspberry flavor gelatin
  1 package (12 ounces) frozen
    unsweetened raspberries

CREAM LAYER
  1 package (3 ounces) cream
    cheese, softened
  ¹/₃ cup confectioners' sugar
  1 teaspoon vanilla
  ¹/₈ teaspoon salt
  1 cup whipping cream,
    whipped

SAUCE
  2 squares (1 ounce each)
    unsweetened baking
    chocolate
  1 tablespoon Butter Flavor
    CRISCO® Stick or
    1 tablespoon Butter
    Flavor CRISCO®
    all-vegetable shortening
  ³/₄ cup confectioners' sugar
  ¹/₈ teaspoon salt
    About 2 tablespoons hot
    milk

1. For crust, prepare and bake 9-inch single crust as directed. Cool crust completely.

2. For raspberry layer, combine granulated sugar, cornstarch and ¹/₈ teaspoon salt in medium saucepan. Gradually stir in water. Cook and stir on medium heat until mixture comes to a boil and is thickened and clear. Add gelatin. Stir until dissolved. Stir in raspberries. Refrigerate until slightly thickened.

3. For cream layer, combine cream cheese, ¹/₃ cup confectioners' sugar, vanilla and ¹/₈ teaspoon salt in medium bowl. Beat at medium speed with electric mixer until smooth. Beat in whipped cream. Spread half of cream mixture on bottom of cooled baked pie crust. Top with half of raspberry mixture. Repeat layers. Refrigerate 1 hour.

4. For sauce, combine chocolate and 1 tablespoon shortening in small microwave-safe bowl. Microwave at 50% (MEDIUM) for 1 minute. Stir. Repeat until melted and smooth. (Or, melt on rangetop in small saucepan on very low heat.) Stir in ³/₄ cup confectioners' sugar and ¹/₈ teaspoon salt until fine crumbs form. Stir in milk, a little at a time, until mixture is of desired consistency. Drizzle over raspberry layer and edge of crust. Refrigerate at least 1 to 2 hours before serving. Refrigerate leftovers.

Makes 1 (9-inch) pie
(8 servings)

Raspberry and Cream Pie

Crisco.com **We cook.**

ARKANSAS'S BEST PUMPKIN PIE

1 unbaked Classic CRISCO®
Single Crust (page 70)

FILLING
1³/₄ cups canned solid-pack
   pumpkin (not pumpkin
   pie filling)
1¹/₄ cups evaporated milk
   2 eggs, beaten
   ³/₄ cup granulated sugar
   1 teaspoon ground cinnamon
   ¹/₄ teaspoon salt

TOPPING
¹/₂ cup all-purpose flour
¹/₃ cup firmly packed brown
   sugar
   3 tablespoons Butter Flavor
   CRISCO® all-vegetable
   shortening
¹/₂ teaspoon ground cinnamon
¹/₈ teaspoon salt
¹/₂ cup chopped pecans
   Sweetened whipped cream
   (optional)
   6 to 8 pecan halves (optional)

1. Heat oven to 350°F.

2. For filling, combine pumpkin,
evaporated milk, eggs, granulated
sugar, 1 teaspoon cinnamon and
¹/₄ teaspoon salt in large bowl. Stir
until smooth and creamy. Pour into
unbaked pie crust.

3. For topping, combine flour,
brown sugar, shortening,
¹/₂ teaspoon cinnamon and
¹/₈ teaspoon salt. Mix with fork or
pastry blender until coarse crumbs

form. Stir in chopped pecans.
Sprinkle evenly over filling.

4. Bake at 350°F for 45 to
55 minutes or until knife inserted
in center comes out clean. Cool to
room temperature before serving.
Garnish with sweetened whipped
cream and pecan halves, if desired.
Makes 1 (9-inch) pie
(8 servings)

Kitchen Hint. . . . . . .

Be sure to only use canned
solid-pack pumpkin and not
pumpkin pie filling in this
recipe. Pumpkin pie filling
already contains spices and
other added ingredients which
will effect the flavor and
texture of your pie.

LIGHT LEMON MERINGUE PIE

CRUST
>   1 unbaked Classic CRISCO®
>   Single Crust (page 70)

FILLING
>   1 cup sugar
>   ⅓ cup cornstarch
>   ⅛ teaspoon salt (optional)
> 1½ cups cold water
>   1 egg yolk, lightly beaten
>   ⅓ cup lemon juice
>   1 teaspoon grated lemon peel

MERINGUE
>   3 egg whites
>   ⅛ teaspoon salt (optional)
>   ¼ cup sugar
>   ½ teaspoon vanilla

1. Heat oven to 375°F.

2. For crust, prick bottom and sides of unbaked pie crust thoroughly with fork (50 times) to prevent shrinkage. Bake at 375°F for 12 to 15 minutes or until lightly browned. *Do not overbake.* Remove from oven. *Reduce oven temperature to 350°F.*

3. For filling, combine sugar, cornstarch and salt in medium saucepan. Gradually stir in water until mixture is well blended. Cook and stir over medium-high heat until sugar mixture comes to a boil. Reduce heat to medium. Cook and stir 5 minutes. Remove from heat.

4. Stir small amount of hot mixture into egg yolk in small bowl. Return mixture to saucepan. Cook and stir for 1 minute. Remove from heat. Stir in lemon juice and lemon peel.

5. For meringue, beat egg whites and salt in small bowl until frothy. Gradually add sugar, beating well after each addition. Beat until stiff, but not dry. Beat in vanilla.

6. Spoon filling into baked pie shell. Spread meringue over filling, sealing meringue to edge of pie shell.

7. Bake at 350°F for 15 minutes or until golden brown. *Do not overbake.* Cool completely on rack. Cut with sharp knife dipped into hot water.
Makes 1 (9-inch) pie
(8 servings)

SPICED CRANBERRY–APPLE SOUR CREAM COBBLER

4 cups cranberries, washed
6 Granny Smith apples, peeled and sliced thin
2 cups firmly packed light brown sugar
1 teaspoon ground cinnamon
1 teaspoon vanilla
1/4 teaspoon ground cloves
2 cups plus 1 tablespoon all-purpose flour, divided
4 tablespoons butter, cut into pieces
2 teaspoons double acting baking powder
1 teaspoon salt
1/2 CRISCO® Stick or 1/2 cup CRISCO® all-vegetable shortening
1 1/2 cups sour cream
2 teaspoons granulated sugar

1. Heat oven to 400°F. Combine cranberries, apples, brown sugar, cinnamon, vanilla, ground cloves and 1 tablespoon flour in 3-quart baking dish; mix evenly. Dot top with butter.

2. Stir together remaining 2 cups flour, baking powder and salt in medium bowl. Cut shortening in using pastry blender or 2 knives until medium-size crumbs form. Add sour cream; blend well. (Dough will be sticky.) Drop dough by spoonfuls on top of fruit mixture. Sprinkle with granulated sugar. Bake at 400°F for 20 to 30 minutes, on middle rack, until top is golden. Serve with cinnamon or vanilla ice cream, if desired. *Makes 6 to 8 servings*

Kitchen Hint. . . . . . .

Lucky enough to have some leftover cobbler? Store it in the refrigerator for up to two days. Reheat, covered, in a 350°F oven until warm.

Spiced Cranberry–Apple Sour Cream Cobbler

BOB'S BEST DEEP-DISH DOUBLE CRUST APPLE PIE

CRUST
   1 unbaked Classic CRISCO®
      Double Crust (page 70)

FILLING
   8 cups sliced, peeled Fuji or
      Gala apples (about
      3 pounds or 8 medium
      apples)
   1 cup sugar
   2 tablespoons all-purpose
      flour
   1/2 teaspoon ground cinnamon
   1/2 teaspoon ground ginger
   1/8 teaspoon ground nutmeg
   1 tablespoon butter or
      margarine, cut into pieces

TOPPING
   1 egg white
   1 tablespoon water
      Sugar

1. For crust, prepare as directed. Roll and press bottom crust into 9- or 9½-inch deep-dish pie plate. *Do not bake.* Heat oven to 375°F.

2. For filling, place apples in large bowl. Combine 1 cup sugar, flour, cinnamon, ginger and nutmeg in small bowl. Sprinkle over apples. Toss to coat. Spoon into unbaked pie crust. Dot with butter. Moisten pastry edge with water.

3. Roll top crust same as bottom. Lift onto filled pie. Trim ½ inch beyond edge of pie plate. Fold top edge under bottom crust. Flute. Cut slits in top crust to allow steam to escape.

4. For topping, beat egg white with water in small bowl until frothy. Brush over top crust. Sprinkle with sugar. Cover edge of pie with foil to prevent overbrowning.

5. Bake at 375°F for 25 minutes. *Do not overbake.* Remove foil. Bake 25 minutes or until filling in center is bubbly and crust is golden brown. Cool to room temperature before serving.

*Makes 1 (9- or 9½-inch)
deep-dish pie (8 servings)*

HONEY CRUNCH PECAN PIE

CRUST
1 unbaked Classic CRISCO®
   Single Crust (page 70)

FILLING
4 eggs, lightly beaten
1 cup light corn syrup
1/4 cup firmly packed brown
   sugar
1/4 cup granulated sugar
2 tablespoons butter or
   margarine, melted
1 tablespoon bourbon
1 teaspoon vanilla
1/2 teaspoon salt
1 cup chopped pecans

TOPPING
1/3 cup firmly packed brown
   sugar
3 tablespoons butter or
   margarine
3 tablespoons honey
1 1/2 cups pecan halves

1. For crust, prepare as directed. *Do not bake.* Heat oven to 350°F.

2. For filling, combine eggs, corn syrup, 1/4 cup brown sugar, granulated sugar, 2 tablespoons butter, bourbon, vanilla and salt in large bowl. Stir in chopped nuts. Mix well. Spoon into unbaked pie crust.

3. Bake at 350°F for 15 minutes. Cover edge with foil to prevent overbrowning. Bake 20 minutes. Remove from oven. Remove foil and save.

4. For topping, combine 1/3 cup brown sugar, 3 tablespoons butter and honey in medium saucepan. Cook about 2 minutes or until sugar dissolves. Add pecan halves. Stir until coated. Spoon over pie. Re-cover edge with foil. Bake 10 to 20 minutes or until topping is bubbly and crust is golden brown. *Do not overbake.* Cool to room temperature before serving. Refrigerate leftover pie.

*Makes 1 (9-inch) pie
(8 servings)*

Kitchen Hint. . . . . .

To make chopping the pecans easier, warm them first. Warm nuts are easier to chop than cold or room temperature nuts. Place 1 cup shelled pecans in a microwavable dish and heat at HIGH about 30 seconds or just until warm; chop as desired.

CHOCOLATE FUDGE PIE

1 unbaked Classic CRISCO®
  Double Crust (page 70)
¼ CRISCO® Stick or ¼ cup
  CRISCO® all-vegetable
  shortening
1 bar (4 ounces) sweet
  baking chocolate
1 can (14 ounces) sweetened
  condensed milk
½ cup all-purpose flour
2 eggs, beaten
1 teaspoon vanilla
¼ teaspoon salt
1 cup flake coconut
1 cup chopped pecans
  Unsweetened whipped
  cream or ice cream

1. Heat oven to 350°F.

2. Melt shortening and chocolate
in heavy saucepan over low heat.
Remove from heat. Stir in sweetened
condensed milk, flour, eggs, vanilla
and salt; mix well. Stir in coconut
and nuts. Pour into unbaked pie
crust.

3. Bake at 350°F for 40 minutes
or until toothpick inserted in center
comes out clean. Cool completely on
cooling rack.

4. Serve with unsweetened whipped
cream or ice cream, if desired.
Refrigerate leftover pie.

Makes 1 (9-inch) pie
(8 servings)

PEACHY BLUEBERRY PIE

1 unbaked Classic CRISCO®
  Double Crust (page 70)
4 cups peeled and thinly
  sliced fresh ripe peaches
1½ cups fresh blueberries,
  washed and well drained
1 cup plus 2 tablespoons
  granulated sugar, divided
2 tablespoons cornstarch
2 teaspoons vanilla
¼ cup milk

1. Heat oven to 350°F. Combine
peaches, blueberries, 1 cup sugar,
cornstarch and vanilla in large
bowl. Mix gently until cornstarch
is dissolved and fruit is well coated.
Pour into unbaked pie crust. Moisten
pastry edge with water. Cover pie
with top crust. Trim ½ inch beyond
edge of pie plate. Fold top edge
under bottom crust; flute. Cut slits in
top of crust to allow steam to escape.

2. Bake at 350°F for about
35 minutes. Remove from oven;
brush top with milk and sprinkle
with 2 tablespoons sugar. Return to
oven and continue to bake for an
additional 15 to 20 minutes or until
peach-blueberry mixture bubbles
and crust is golden. Let rest
10 minutes before serving.

Makes 1 (9-inch) pie
(8 servings)

Chocolate Fudge Pie

Crisco.com We cook.

CLASSIC CRISCO® DOUBLE CRUST

2 cups all-purpose flour
1 teaspoon salt
¾ CRISCO® Stick or ¾ cup CRISCO® all-vegetable shortening
5 tablespoons cold water (or more as needed)

1. Spoon flour into measuring cup and level. Combine flour and salt in medium bowl.

2. Cut in ¾ cup shortening using pastry blender or 2 knives until all flour is blended to form pea-size chunks.

3. Sprinkle with water, 1 tablespoon at a time. Toss lightly with fork until dough forms a ball. Divide dough in half.

4. Press dough between hands to form 5- to 6-inch "pancake." Flour rolling surface and rolling pin lightly. Roll both halves of dough into circle. Trim one circle of dough 1 inch larger than upside-down pie plate. Carefully remove trimmed dough. Set aside to reroll and use for pastry cutout garnish, if desired.

5. Fold dough into quarters. Unfold and press into pie plate. Trim edge even with plate. Add desired filling to unbaked crust. Moisten pastry edge with water. Lift top crust onto filled pie. Trim ½ inch beyond edge of pie plate. Fold top edge under bottom crust. Flute. Cut slits in top crust to allow steam to escape. Follow baking directions given for that recipe.

Makes 1 (9-inch) double crust

CLASSIC CRISCO® SINGLE CRUST

1⅓ cups all-purpose flour
½ teaspoon salt
½ CRISCO® Stick or ½ cup CRISCO® all-vegetable shortening
3 tablespoons cold water

1. Spoon flour into measuring cup and level. Combine flour and salt in medium bowl.

2. Cut in ½ cup shortening using pastry blender or 2 knives until all flour is blended to form pea-size chunks.

3. Sprinkle with water, 1 tablespoon at a time. Toss lightly with fork until dough forms a ball.

4. Press dough between hands to form 5- to 6-inch "pancake." Flour rolling surface and rolling pin lightly. Roll dough into circle. Trim circle 1 inch larger than upside-down pie plate. Carefully remove trimmed dough. Set aside to reroll and use for pastry cutout garnish, if desired.

5. Fold dough into quarters. Unfold and press into pie plate. Fold edge under. Flute.

6. For recipes using a baked pie crust, heat oven to 425°F. Prick bottom and side thoroughly with fork (50 times) to prevent shrinkage. Bake at 425°F for 10 to 15 minutes or until lightly browned.

7. For recipes using an unbaked pie crust, follow directions given for that recipe.

Makes 1 (9-inch) single crust

Crisco.com **We cook.**

APPLE–
CRANBERRY–
RASPBERRY PIE

1 unbaked Classic CRISCO®
    Double Crust (page 70)
2 cups chopped, peeled
    Granny Smith apples
    (about $2/3$ pound or
    2 medium)
2 cups whole cranberries,
    coarsely chopped
1 package (10 ounces) frozen
    dry pack raspberries,
    thawed
$1^1/2$ cups sugar
3 tablespoons quick-cooking
    tapioca
$1/2$ teaspoon ground cinnamon
$1/4$ teaspoon salt
$1/4$ teaspoon almond extract
    Half-and-half or milk
    Sugar

1. Heat oven to 375°F. Combine apples, cranberries and raspberries in large bowl. Combine sugar, tapioca, cinnamon, salt and almond extract in small bowl. Add to fruit mixture; toss well. Spoon into unbaked pie crust. Fold edge under; flute.

2. Trim top crust dough to circle $2^1/2$ inches smaller than upside-down pie plate. Cut a spiral strip starting from outside, about $3/4$ inch wide. Flip onto filling. Gently separate strip with knife tip to form opened spiral.

3. Brush spiral with half-and-half. Sprinkle with sugar. Cover edge with foil to prevent over browning. Bake at 375°F for 25 minutes. Remove foil. Bake an additional 25 to 35 minutes or until filling in center is bubbly. Cool until barely warm or room temperature before serving.

Makes 1 (9-inch) pie
(8 servings)

APPLE–WALNUT "PIZZA PIE"

PIZZA CRUST
2½ cups all-purpose flour
4 tablespoons granulated
    sugar
1¼ teaspoons salt
½ cup CRISCO® Canola Oil
4 tablespoons milk
½ teaspoons almond extract

PIZZA TOPPING
4 medium Granny Smith
    apples (peeled, cored,
    quartered and sliced thin)
½ cup chopped walnuts
⅓ cup firmly packed light
    brown sugar
3 tablespoons raisins
1½ teaspoons ground
    cinnamon
½ tablespoon vanilla
6 tablespoons apple butter
½ cup grated coconut

1. Heat oven to 400°F. For pizza crust, combine flour, granulated sugar and salt in large bowl; mix well. Whisk together oil, milk and almond extract in small bowl until well blended. Slowly pour oil mixture into flour mixture while stirring with fork until mixed well and crumbly.

2. Spray 12¼-inch pizza pan with CRISCO® No-Stick Cooking Spray. Press crumb mixture with fingers firmly onto bottom and side of pan. Bake at 400°F for about 10 minutes or until golden brown; remove from oven. *Reduce oven temperature to 350°F.*

3. For pizza topping, combine apples, walnuts, brown sugar, raisins, cinnamon and vanilla in large bowl; mix well.

4. Spread apple butter evenly over baked pizza crust. Place apple mixture on top. Sprinkle with coconut "cheese." Bake at 350°F for 25 to 30 minutes. Remove from oven and serve warm or at room temperature. Cut into "pizza slices" and garnish with whipped cream.
Makes 6 to 8 servings

Kitchen Hint. . . . . . .

Apple butter is a preserve made by slowly cooking apples, sugar, spices and cider together. It is thick and has a dark brown color. It is great as a spread on breads and a great accompaniment to peanut butter.

Apple–Walnut "Pizza Pie"

CHERRY CHEESECAKE PIE

CRUST
 1 unbaked Classic CRISCO®
   Single Crust (page 70)

FILLING
 2 cans (16 ounces each)
   pitted red tart cherries
   packed in water
 ¼ cup reserved cherry liquid
 ½ cup sugar
 1 tablespoon cornstarch
 1 teaspoon lemon juice
 ⅛ teaspoon almond extract

TOPPING
 1½ packages (8 ounces each)
   cream cheese, softened
 ½ cup sugar
 2 eggs
 ½ teaspoon vanilla
   Baked pastry cutouts
   (optional)

1. For crust, prepare as directed. *Do not bake.* Reserve dough scraps for decoration, if desired. Heat oven to 425°F.

2. For filling, drain cherries in large strainer over bowl, reserving ¼ cup liquid. Combine ½ cup sugar and cornstarch in large bowl. Stir in reserved ¼ cup cherry liquid, lemon juice and almond extract. Stir in cherries. Spoon into unbaked pie crust. Bake at 425°F for 15 minutes. Remove from oven.

3. For topping, combine cream cheese, ½ cup sugar, eggs and vanilla in medium bowl. Beat at medium speed of electric mixer until smooth. Spoon over hot cherry filling.

4. *Reduce oven temperature to 350°F.* Return pie to oven. Bake for 25 minutes or until topping is set. *Do not overbake.* Cool to room temperature before serving. Garnish with baked pastry cutouts, if desired. Refrigerate leftovers.

*Makes 1 (9-inch) pie
(8 servings)*

Kitchen Hint. . . . . . .

To make pastry cut-outs, roll dough scraps out on lightly floured surface. Using small cookie cutters, cut dough into desired shapes. Decorate top of pie with shapes before baking.

Seasonal Fruit Cobbler

APPLE
5 cups sliced, peeled cooking apples (about 1²/₃ pounds or 5 medium)
1 cup sugar
¹/₃ cup water or apple juice
2 tablespoons butter or margarine
2 tablespoons all-purpose flour
¹/₂ teaspoon ground cinnamon
¹/₄ teaspoon ground nutmeg

BLUEBERRY
4 cups blueberries
¹/₂ cup sugar
1 tablespoon cornstarch
1 teaspoon lemon juice
1 teaspoon grated lemon peel

CHERRY
4 cups pitted fresh or thawed frozen dry pack red tart cherries
1¹/₄ cups sugar
3 tablespoons cornstarch
¹/₄ teaspoon ground cinnamon
¹/₄ teaspoon almond extract
¹/₂ cup sugar
¹/₃ cup water
1 tablespoon cornstarch
¹/₄ teaspoon ground cinnamon
Dash of ground nutmeg

BISCUIT TOPPING
1 cup all-purpose flour
2 tablespoons sugar
1¹/₂ teaspoons baking powder
¹/₄ teaspoon salt
¹/₄ cup CRISCO® all-vegetable shortening
1 egg, slightly beaten
¹/₄ cup milk
¹/₂ teaspoon vanilla

1. Select fruit recipe. Heat oven to 400°F. Combine fruit ingredients in large saucepan. Cook and stir over medium heat until mixture comes to a boil and thickens. Stir and simmer 1 minute. Pour into 8-inch square glass baking dish or 2-quart baking dish. Bake 25 minutes.

2. For biscuit topping, combine flour, sugar, baking powder and salt in medium bowl. Cut in shortening with pastry blender or 2 knives until crumbs form. Combine egg, milk and vanilla in small bowl. Add all at once to flour mixture. Stir just until moistened. Remove baking dish from oven.

3. Drop biscuit mixture in 8 mounds on top of hot fruit. Bake at 400°F for 20 minutes or until golden brown. Serve warm with cream or ice cream, if desired.

Makes 8 servings

Ethnic Holidays

PLUM STREUSEL

PLUM FILLING
- ½ cup firmly packed light brown sugar
- 3 tablespoons cornstarch
- ½ teaspoon ground nutmeg
- 2½ pounds ripe plums, pitted and sliced ½ inch thick

STREUSEL
- 1 cup all-purpose flour
- ½ Butter Flavor CRISCO® Stick or ½ cup Butter Flavor CRISCO® all-vegetable shortening
- ½ cup firmly packed light brown sugar
- 1 teaspoon ground cinnamon
- 1 teaspoon vanilla
- ¼ teaspoon salt

1. Heat oven to 350°F. Spray 3-quart shallow baking dish with CRISCO® No-Stick Cooking Spray; set aside.

2. For filling, combine ½ cup brown sugar, cornstarch and nutmeg in large bowl; mix well. Add plums; stir gently to coat evenly. Place in prepared pan.

3. For streusel, combine flour, shortening, ½ cup brown sugar, cinnamon, vanilla and salt in large bowl. Mix with fork until mixture is combined and just crumbly. *Do not overmix.* Sprinkle over fruit mixture.

4. Bake at 350°F for 45 minutes or until streusel top is crisp. Cool about 10 minutes; serve warm with whipped cream or ice cream.

Makes 6 to 8 servings

Crisco.com We cook.

MA'MOUL
(DATE PASTRIES)

FILLING
- 1 pound chopped pitted dates
- ½ cup water
- ¼ cup granulated sugar
- 1 teaspoon almond extract
- 2 tablespoons fresh grated orange peel
- ½ teaspoon ground cinnamon

PASTRY
- 1 Butter Flavor CRISCO® Stick or 1 cup Butter Flavor CRISCO® all-vegetable shortening
- ¼ cup granulated sugar
- 3 tablespoons milk
- 1 tablespoon rosewater or water
- 2 cups all-purpose flour
  Confectioners' sugar

1. For filling, combine dates, water, ¼ cup sugar and almond extract in small saucepan. Bring to a boil over medium-high heat. Reduce heat to low; simmer 4 to 5 minutes, stirring often, until mixture becomes thick paste. Stir in orange peel and cinnamon. Remove from heat; cool.

2. Heat oven to 300°F.

3. For pastry, combine shortening and ¼ cup sugar in large bowl. Beat at medium speed with electric mixer until well blended. Beat in milk and rosewater. Beat in flour, ¼ cup at a time, until well blended. Knead dough in bowl until dough holds together and is easy to shape.

4. Pinch off walnut-size piece of dough. Roll into ball. Pinch sides up to form pot shape. Fill center with level tablespoonful of date filling. Pinch dough closed; press to seal. Slightly flatten and smooth top. Place on ungreased baking sheets about 1 inch apart.

5. Bake at 300°F for 16 to 20 minutes or until firm and set. *Do not allow pastries to brown.* Cool on baking sheets 3 minutes; transfer to cooling rack. Sprinkle with confectioners' sugar while still warm. Cool completely.

Makes about 2½ dozen pastries

Background. . . . . . .

These cookies are traditionally served in Syria during the Easter Holiday.

Ma'moul (Date Pastries)

VANILKOVE ROHLICKY (VANILLA CRESCENTS)

½ Butter Flavor CRISCO® Stick
or ½ cup Butter Flavor
CRISCO® all-vegetable
shortening
½ cup granulated sugar
2 cups all-purpose flour
1½ cups ground almonds
1 teaspoon vanilla
¼ teaspoon ground allspice
¼ teaspoon salt
Confectioners' sugar

1. Combine shortening and granulated sugar in large bowl. Beat at medium speed with electric mixer until well blended. Beat in flour, ½ cup at a time. Beat in almonds, vanilla, allspice and salt until well blended. Continue to beat until dough is just stiff. Shape dough into ball. Wrap in plastic wrap and refrigerate 2 hours.

2. Heat oven to 350°F. Spray cookie sheets with CRISCO® No-Stick Cooking Spray; set aside.

3. Pinch off round pieces of dough about 1½ inches in diameter. Roll each piece of dough, on floured surface, into 2½×1-inch log. Shape into crescent; place on prepared cookie sheets about 1 inch apart.

4. Bake at 350°F for 15 to 18 minutes or until lightly brown. Cool on cookie sheets 4 minutes; transfer to cooling racks. Dust with confectioners' sugar.
Makes about 3 dozen cookies

Background. . . . . . .

These cookies are a very important part of Christmas in Czechoslovakia. The story is that when Czech president Vaclav Havel was allowed food after being in the hospital's intensive care unit for 10 days during the holidays, he requested Vanilkove Rohlicky stating that "without this treat it would not be Christmas."

Crisco.com We cook.

ROASTED ALMONDS

2 tablespoons CRISCO® Canola Oil, divided
1 pound whole blanched almonds
2 teaspoons ground cinnamon
Confectioners' sugar

1. Heat 1 tablespoon oil in large skillet over medium heat until hot. Add ½ pound almonds. Cook and stir until evenly browned. Sprinkle with 1 teaspoon cinnamon; stir well. Place on paper towels to drain. Dust with confectioners' sugar to taste.

2. Repeat with remaining ingredients.   *Makes 1 pound nuts*

Background......

This traditionally African dish is great as a dessert or snack.

KLU AY TOD (BANANA FRITTERS)

2 cups self-rising flour
¼ cup granulated sugar
1 teaspoon baking powder
½ teaspoon salt
1½ cups water
2 large eggs, beaten
4 large bananas, slightly under ripe
CRISCO® Canola Oil
¼ cup honey

1. Combine flour, sugar, baking powder and salt in large bowl. Whisk in water until mixture is smooth. Whisk in eggs; mix well.

2. Cut bananas into 1-inch pieces. Place in batter; stir gently to coat pieces thoroughly.

3. Pour oil about 1¼ inch deep into large skillet. Heat over medium-high heat until hot. Do not allow to smoke. Add battered banana pieces, keeping them separated. Cook on one side until golden; turn pieces and cook until other side is golden. Continue to cook pieces, turning often, until light brown and crisp. Remove and drain on paper towels. Place on large serving platter; drizzle with honey. Serve warm and with vanilla ice cream, if desired.
Makes 4 to 6 servings

Background......

This is Thailand's most popular dessert and is found at almost every festive occasion.

PASSOVER HONEY–WALNUT–APRICOT TART

TART SHELL
- 1 cup matzo meal
- 5 tablespoons Butter Flavor CRISCO® all-vegetable shortening
- ¼ cup water
- 2 teaspoons honey

FILLING
- ½ Butter Flavor CRISCO® Stick or ½ cup Butter Flavor CRISCO® all-vegetable shortening
- ⅓ cup honey
- ¼ cup granulated sugar
- 1½ cups chopped walnuts
- 1 cup chopped dried apricots
- 1 tablespoon orange juice
- 1 teaspoon vanilla
- ½ teaspoon fresh grated orange peel

1. For shell, place matzo meal in bowl of food processor, fitted with metal blade. Process until very fine. Add 5 tablespoons shortening, water and 2 teaspoons honey; pulse until ball forms. *Do not over process.*

2. Sprinkle work surface with additional matzo meal. Roll dough into 10-inch circle. Lightly spray 9-inch removable bottom tart pan with CRISCO® No-Stick Cooking Spray. Press dough into bottom and up side of pan. Refrigerate at least 45 minutes.

3. Heat oven to 400°F.

4. For filling, combine ½ cup shortening, ⅓ cup honey and sugar in small saucepan. Bring to a boil over medium-high heat. Add walnuts, apricots, orange juice, vanilla and orange peel. Boil 1 minute, stirring constantly. Remove from heat.

5. Place tart pan on baking sheet. Pour filling into crust. Bake at 400°F for 20 minutes or until filling is set and crust is lightly browned. Cool on cooling rack.

Makes 8 to 10 servings

Background. . . . . .

Passover always occurs on the fifteenth day of Nisan, the first month in the Hebrew calendar. During Passover, foods with flour and leavening (except matzo) are not eaten. This tart recipe uses matzo instead of flour to adhere to the traditions of Passover.

Passover Honey–Walnut–Apricot Tart

Crisco.com **We cook.**

SFINCE DI SAN GIUSEPPE (ST. JOSEPH'S RICOTTA PUFFS)

FILLING
- 1 pound ricotta cheese, drained
- ½ cup confectioners' sugar
- 4 ounces grated dark chocolate
- ¼ cup candied fruit, finely chopped
- 1 teaspoon orange extract
- 1 teaspoon vanilla

PUFFS
- 1 cup water
- ½ Butter Flavor CRISCO® Stick or ½ cup Butter Flavor CRISCO® all-vegetable shortening
- 1 tablespoon granulated sugar
- ½ teaspoon salt
- 1 cup sifted all-purpose flour
- 4 large eggs, beaten
- 1 teaspoon fresh grated lemon peel
- 1 teaspoon fresh grated orange peel
- Confectioners' sugar

1. For filling, combine all filling ingredients in large bowl; mix well. Refrigerate while making puffs.

2. For puffs, heat oven to 450°F. Combine water, shortening, granulated sugar and salt in medium saucepan. Bring to a boil over medium-high heat; stir well.

Add flour, stirring vigorously, until mixture leaves sides of pan. Remove from heat; let cool.

3. Slowly add eggs, beating vigorously, to cooled flour mixture. Add lemon and orange peel; mix well.

4. Spray baking sheets with CRISCO® No-Stick Cooking Spray. Drop tablespoonfuls of batter 2 inches apart onto baking sheets.

5. Bake at 450°F for 15 minutes. *Reduce oven temperature to 350°F.* Bake an additional 15 to 20 minutes or until golden. Cool completely on cooling rack.

6. To assemble, cut puffs in half horizontally. Spoon ricotta filling into bottom half. Cover with top half. Drizzle with melted chocolate, if desired.   *Makes about 18 puffs*

Background. . . . . . .

This dessert is traditionally made on March 19, the feast day of St. Joseph. They appear in bakeries weeks before and are still there weeks after March 19. These delightful treats are delicious any time of the year.

*Sfince Di San Giuseppe
(St. Joseph's Ricotta Puffs)*

POLVORONES (DUST BALLS)

1 Butter Flavor CRISCO® Stick or 1 cup Butter Flavor CRISCO® all-vegetable shortening
2 cups confectioners' sugar, divided
2 teaspoons vanilla
2 cups all-purpose flour
½ teaspoon baking soda
⅛ teaspoon salt
2 cups finely chopped hazelnuts (also called filberts)

1. Heat oven to 350°F.

2. Combine shortening, 1 cup confectioners' sugar and vanilla in large bowl. Beat at medium speed with electric mixer until well blended.

3. Combine flour, baking soda and salt in medium bowl. Add to creamed mixture; mix well. Stir in hazelnuts and mix well.

4. Roll dough into walnut-size balls and place on ungreased cookie sheets about 1½ inches apart. Bake at 350°F for 15 minutes or until edges begin to brown lightly. Cool on cookies sheets until cool enough to handle, but still warm. While still warm, roll in remaining 1 cup confectioners' sugar; place on cooling racks to cool completely.
Makes about 4 dozen cookies

Background. . . . . . .

These cookies are often served at weddings, baptisms and other celebrations. Polvorone means dust ball in Spanish, referring to the powdered sugar on them. They are also known as Mexican wedding cakes and Russian tea cakes.

Crisco.com We cook.

MANGO BREAD

2 cups all-purpose flour
1½ cups granulated sugar
½ teaspoon salt
2 teaspoons baking soda
1 teaspoon baking powder
1 teaspoon ground cinnamon
¼ teaspoon ground ginger
¾ cup CRISCO® Canola Oil
3 eggs, beaten
1 teaspoon vanilla
2 cups fresh ripe mango,
    peeled and diced
¾ cup golden raisins
¾ cup macadamia nuts,
    chopped
½ cup grated coconut

1. Heat oven to 350°F. Spray two 9×5-inch loaf pans with CRISCO® No-Stick Cooking Spray. Dust with flour; set aside.

2. Combine flour, sugar, salt, baking soda, baking powder, cinnamon and ginger in large bowl.

3. Combine oil, eggs and vanilla in medium bowl; mix well. Add to flour mixture; mix well. Fold in mango, raisins, nuts and coconut.

4. Pour batter into prepared loaf pans. Bake at 350°F for 45 to 60 minutes or until wooden pick inserted into center of each loaf comes out clean and loaves are golden. Cool in pans 10 minutes. Turn out onto cooling rack; cool completely.

Makes 6 to 8 servings per loaf

Background. . . . . . .

A tradition in the Hawaiian Islands is to bring a loaf of bread to friends and neighbors when you are invited to their home. This bread is often given as a gift to new neighbors as a sign of welcome.

GINGERBREAD CAKE WITH LEMON SAUCE

CAKE
- ¼ Butter Flavor CRISCO® Stick or ¼ cup Butter Flavor CRISCO® all-vegetable shortening
- ¼ cup firmly packed light brown sugar
- ¼ cup granulated sugar
- 1 large egg, lightly beaten
- ½ cup buttermilk
- ¼ cup light molasses
- 1 cup all-purpose flour
- 2 teaspoons ground ginger
- 1 teaspoon ground cinnamon
- ½ teaspoon baking soda
- ¼ teaspoon ground cloves
- ¼ teaspoon freshly grated nutmeg
- ¼ teaspoon salt

LEMON SAUCE
- ½ cup granulated sugar
- ¼ cup unsalted butter
- 3 tablespoons fresh lemon juice
- 1 teaspoon vanilla

1. Heat oven to 375°F. Lightly spray 8-inch square or round cake pan with CRISCO® No-Stick Cooking Spray; set aside.

2. For cake, combine shortening, brown sugar and ¼ cup granulated sugar in large bowl. Beat at medium speed with electric mixer until well blended. Beat in egg, buttermilk and molasses until well blended.

3. Combine flour, ginger, cinnamon, baking soda, cloves, nutmeg and salt in medium bowl.

Add to creamed mixture; mix well. Pour batter into prepared pan.

4. Bake at 375°F for 20 to 25 minutes or until wooden pick inserted into center comes out clean. Cool in pan 15 minutes. Turn out onto cooling rack.

5. For Lemon Sauce, combine all ingredients in small saucepan. Bring to a boil over medium-high heat, stirring constantly. Reduce heat to low and simmer 5 minutes or until sauce is slightly thickened. Serve sauce over each slice of cake.

Makes 6 to 8 servings

Background. . . . . . .

The history of gingerbread in England dates back to the Middle Ages when fair ladies presented it to knights before they went into tournament battle.

Gingerbread Cake with Lemon Sauce

Crisco.com We cook.

TARTE AU SUCRE (SUGAR TART)

1 unbaked 9-inch Classic CRISCO® Single Crust* (page 70)
¾ cup firmly packed brown sugar
¾ cup granulated sugar
½ cup ground almonds
2 large eggs, beaten
1½ tablespoons all-purpose flour
½ teaspoon fresh grated nutmeg
½ cup plus 1 tablespoon heavy cream
½ teaspoon almond extract
½ teaspoon vanilla
2 tablespoons unsalted butter, cut into small pieces

*Prepare pie crust using Butter Flavor CRISCO® all-vegetable shortening.

1. Heat oven to 350°F. Lightly spray 9-inch removable bottom tart pan with CRISCO® No-Stick Cooking Spray. Press pie crust dough onto bottom and up side of pan; refrigerate.

2. Combine brown sugar, granulated sugar, almonds, eggs, flour and nutmeg in large bowl until well blended. Add cream, almond extract and vanilla until well blended. Place tart pan on baking sheet; pour in filling. Dot evenly with butter.

3. Bake at 350°F for 25 to 30 minutes or until filling is light golden color, puffs up and is just set. Cool on cooling rack. Serve at room temperature. *Makes 8 servings*

Background. . . . . . .

This tart is a favorite for home entertaining in Belgium.

Crisco.com We cook.

Bizcochos (Holiday Cookies)

1³/₄ cups granulated sugar, divided
1 teaspoon ground cinnamon
¹/₂ teaspoon ground cloves
¹/₄ teaspoon ground nutmeg
1 cup CRISCO® all-vegetable shortening
2 egg yolks
3 ounces orange juice
1 teaspoon vanilla
1 teaspoon almond extract
1¹/₂ cups all-purpose flour

1. Heat oven to 350°F. Combine 1 cup sugar, cinnamon, cloves and nutmeg in shallow dish or pie pan; set aside.

2. Combine shortening and remaining ³/₄ cup sugar in large bowl. Beat at medium speed with electric mixer until well blended. Beat in egg yolks, orange juice, vanilla and almond extract. Stir flour into creamed mixture until well blended.

3. Roll dough out to ¹/₄ inch thick. Cut out with cookie cutters and place on ungreased cookie sheets. Bake at 350°F for 12 to 15 minutes or until golden. Cool slightly on cookie sheets. Gently and carefully dredge cookies in sugar and spice mixture while still warm. Place on cooling racks.

Makes about 4 dozen cookies

Background. . . . . .

These cookies are served for holidays and special occasions. They work well for children's birthday parties when they have been cut out with decorative cookie cutters.

BERLINERKRANSER (LITTLE WREATHS)

1 Butter Flavor CRISCO® Stick or 1 cup Butter Flavor CRISCO® all-vegetable shortening
1 cup confectioners' sugar
2 large hard boiled egg yolks, mashed
2 large eggs, separated
1 teaspoon vanilla
1 teaspoon almond extract
2¼ cups all-purpose flour
    Green colored sugar crystals
12 red candied cherries, cut into quarters

1. Combine shortening and confectioners' sugar in large bowl. Beat at medium speed with electric mixer until well blended. Beat in hard boiled egg yolks, uncooked egg yolks, vanilla and almond extract. Beat in flour, ¼ cup at a time, until well blended. Cover and refrigerate 3 hours.

2. Let dough stand at room temperature until it becomes easy to handle.

3. Heat oven to 350°F. Divide dough into 2 equal portions. Cut each portion into 24 equal pieces. Roll each piece of dough into 5-inch long rope. Form each rope into wreath or loop 1½ inches apart on ungreased cookie sheet, overlapping both ends. Brush each wreath with beaten egg white; sprinkle with colored sugar crystals. Lightly press cherry piece into top of each wreath.

4. Bake at 350°F for 10 to 12 minutes or until edges are lightly browned. Cool on cookie sheets 3 minutes; transfer to cooling racks.
Makes about 4 dozen cookies

Background. . . . . . .

These wreath shaped cookies are a Norwegian holiday favorite for the family to bake together.

Crisco.com We cook.